Mu

Haydn Richard
Junior English   1

Ginn and Company Ltd

Acknowledgements

Grateful acknowledgement is made to the following
for permission to use copyright material:

The Vulture

page 18 By Hilaire Belloc from *Cautionary Verses*
By kind permission of the publishers G. Duckworth & Co
Ltd.

The Alchemist

18 By A. A. Milne from *The World of
Christopher Robin*.
By kind permission of the publishers Methuen Children's
Books Ltd

Designed by Michael Soderberg

Illustrated by Barry Rowe, Martin White
and David Atkinson

© Haydn Richards 1965
Revised edition 1981
Twentieth impression 1994   029407

ISBN 0 602 22550 7 (without answers)
ISBN 0 602 22616 3 (with answers)

Published by Ginn and Company Ltd
Prebendal House, Parson's Fee,
Aylesbury, Bucks HP20 2QZ

Filmset by Filmtype Services Limited, Scarborough
Printed in Great Britain at the University Press, Cambridge

Preface

The main aim of Haydn Richards Junior English is to enable the pupil to work alone, as far as is possible. For this reason complete lists of the words needed to answer the various exercises are given. Being thus provided with the necessary tools the pupil should experience little difficulty in doing the work.

The course provides ample and varied practice in all the English topics usually taught in the Junior School. Such simple grammatical terms as are essential to the understanding of the language are introduced at appropriate stages, together with simple definitions, lucid explanations and easy examples.

The meaning of every proverb and idiom dealt with is given, so that these may be used correctly in both writing and conversation.

A noteworthy feature of each book in the series is the detailed Contents, facilitating reference to any particular topic by the teacher and the older pupils.

In addition to teaching and testing such topics as Parts of Speech, Opposites, Synonyms, Homophones, Punctuation, Sentence Linkage and Structure, Direct and Indirect Speech, etc., the course includes verbal intelligence exercises designed to stimulate clear thinking, so that by the end of the fourth year the pupil who has worked steadily through the course is well equipped for any entrance examination.

H.R.

Contents

Usage								
a, an	3							
as, has	41							
did, done	69							
do, does	52							
has, have	46							
is, are	31							
is, his	41							
saw, seen	88							
to, too, two	23							
was, were	31							
Verbs	5	7	13	29	33	34	39	56
Verbal intelligence	40	76						
Words with more than one meaning	47							

The game of I spy

A   Do you know the game of **I Spy**?
Look at the first picture.
I spy with my little eye
Something beginning with **c**.

1   c _ _

This is a **cup**, so you write the word **cup**.
Now do the same with the other pictures.

2   p _ _   3   b _ _ _   4   s _ _ _

5   d _ _   6   l _ _   7   t _ _ _

8   f _ _ _   9   j _ _   10   e _ _

B   Which word fills the gap?

1   A hen laid the ___

• 2   The ___ can bark.

3   A ___ lives in water.

4   A ___ is worn on the foot.

1

Names of things

bag   drum
bed   lamp
book   pen
clock   spoon
door   tap

A Write in order, 1 to 10, the names of the things in the pictures. Look at the list of words on the left.

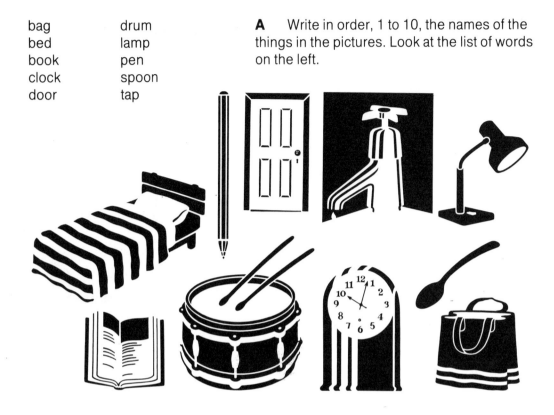

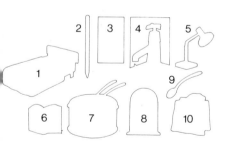

The words you have written are the **names** of things. We call such words **naming words**.

B What am I?

1 You beat me with two sticks.

2 You lie on me when you go to sleep.

3 I can give light when it is dark.

4 You open me when you enter a room.

5 You carry all your shopping in me.

6 You look at me when you read.

7 You come to me for water.

8 People use me to stir their tea.

9 You may use me when you write.

10 I tell you the time.

Using a and an

apple   envelope
arrow   iron
axe   onion
eggcup   oven

A Write the names of these things, putting **an** in front of each. The words you need are in the list on the left.

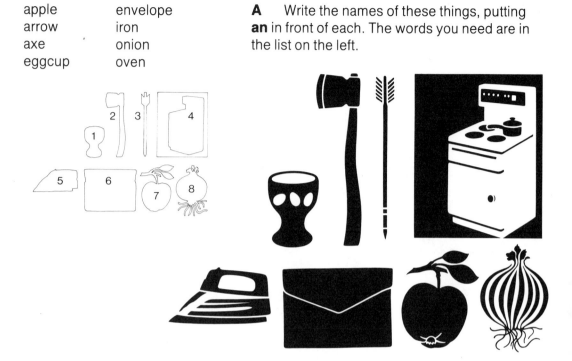

Always write **an** before words beginning with

a e i o u

Always write **a** before words beginning with other letters.

B Write **a** or **an** before each of these words.

1 ____ clock   9 ____ elephant

2 ____ armchair 10 ____ ostrich

3 ____ orchard   11 ____ eagle

4 ____ book   12 ____ hoop

5 ____ pen   13 ____ desk

6 ____ arch   14 ____ island

7 ____ tree   15 ____ umbrella

8 ____ door

Numbers

•	1 one	
• •	2 two	
• • •	3 three	
• • • •	4 four	
• • • • •	5 five	
• • • • • •	6 six	
• • • • • • •	7 seven	
• • • • • • • •	8 eight	
• • • • • • • • •	9 nine	
• • • • • • • • • •	10 ten	

____ cats
Draw five cats.

____ spoons
Draw four spoons.

____ trees
Draw one tree.

____ car
Draw two cars.

____ apples
Draw three apples.

____ eggs
Draw seven eggs.

____ flowers
Draw nine flowers.

____ pencils
Draw ten pencils.

____ mugs
Draw eight mugs.

____ bottles
Draw six bottles.

4

Doing words

eating   jumping
drinking   reading
fishing   sleeping
flying   washing

A   What are they doing?
Make a list of the words. Number them
from 1 to 8.

B   Write the word which fills each gap.

1 The man is ____ his car.

2 The boy is ____ under the tree.

3 The two boys are ____ .

4 The girl is ____ an apple.

5 The woman is ____ a book.

6 The dog is ____ over a log.

7 The birds are ____ high.

8 The cat is ____ milk.

C   Add **-ing** to each of these words.

1 call	5 pull	9 sing
2 draw	6 see	10 bark
3 do	7 hear	11 teach
4 try	8 rain	12 feel

Pam's pet

Pam's pet is a cat named Punch. Punch has a coat of soft black fur. Pam gives him milk every day. He laps it up with his long pink tongue. Then he purrs to show that he is happy.

He often sits on the rug by the fire. There he washes his face with his soft paws. His claws are very sharp, but he does not scratch Pam. Punch keeps mice away from the house.

Copy the sentences.
Fill each space with the right word.

1 Pam's cat is ____ in colour.

2 When Punch is ____ he purrs.

3 Every day Pam gives her cat some ____ .

4 He ____ it up with his ____ tongue.

5 Punch ____ sits on the ____ by the ____ .

6 He washes his ____ with his ____ .

7 His claws are very ____ .

8 Punch keeps ____ away from the ____ .

More doing words

A   Look at the pictures.
Make a list of the doing words. Number them from 1 to 8.

B   Use the words in the list on the left to fill these gaps.

When **-ing** is added to a doing word ending with **e**, the **e** is dropped.

dance	dancing
dive	diving
drive	driving
hide	hiding
ride	riding
skate	skating
wave	waving
write	writing

1 Roger likes ___ his new pony.

2 Ben was ___ in the bushes.

3 We saw Pam ___ to us across the road.

4 Angela uses pen and ink when she is ___ .

5 Stephen passed his ___ test first time.

6 Michael loved ___ off the high board.

7 Kate takes tap ___ lessons every Tuesday.

8 People were ___ on the frozen pond.

7

Telling sentences

Read this sentence.

A cat has sharp claws.

This sentence tells us something about a cat.

It is called a **telling** sentence.

Every telling sentence must end with a **full stop**.

A Copy these sentences and put a full stop at the end of each.

1 Butter is made from milk

2 Honey is made by bees

3 Sugar has a sweet taste

4 The school bus was late today

5 Mary had dinner at school

6 I put some coal on the fire

7 We go blackberrying in the autumn

8 The crocus is a spring flower

9 The elephant has a long trunk

10 A young cat is called a kitten

B Now write one telling sentence about each of these things.

1 a cow

2 your home

3 any tree

4 coal

5 your toys

6 any bird

Asking sentences

Some sentences ask a question.

What is your name?

How old are you?

Where do you live?

Every asking sentence must end with a **question mark**.

A Copy these sentences and put a question mark at the end of each.

1 How are you today

2 Why were you late this morning

3 Where did you put the sweets

4 When are you coming to see me

5 Who told you that I was ill

6 Which of these toys do you like best

7 Will you come to the circus with me

8 Did you remember to post the letter

9 Have you seen John

10 Can you tell me the way

B Now write one asking sentence about each of these things.

1 the time
2 the weather
3 a book
4 a farm
5 money
6 clothes

Capital letters beginning a sentence

Every sentence, both telling and asking, must begin with a **capital letter**.

Small letters	a	b	c	d	e	f	g	h	i	j
Capital letters	A	B	C	D	E	F	G	H	I	J

A   Copy these sentences.
Begin each with a capital letter.

Put a **full stop** at the end of each **telling** sentence.

Put a **question mark** at the end of each **asking** sentence.

1   honey is sweet

2   the sun sets in the west

3   do you like nuts

4   a rabbit has soft fur

5   when will you be ready

6   keep off the grass

7   this meat is very tender

8   are you going shopping

9   look where you are going

10   what is the right time

B   Write six sentences about the rabbit.
Say something about –

1	its fur	4	its teeth
2	its ears	5	its whiskers
3	its tail	6	its home

The alphabet

This is the alphabet.

a b c d e f g h i j k l m
n o p q r s t u v w x y z

You should learn the alphabet well.

From these twenty-six letters all our words are made.

A

1 What is the fifth letter?

2 Write the last letter of all.

3 Which letter comes next after **s**?

4 Which letter comes just before **h**?

5 Write the letter which comes between **k** and **m**.

6 Write the two letters on either side of **e**.

7 Which letter is next but one after **q**?

8 Which letter is next but one before **j**?

9 What are the missing letters?
m n   p q r   t u   w x

10 What word do the missing letters spell?
a   c d   f   h

These letters are jumbled up:
c e a d b

Now they are in the right **a b c** order:
a b c d e

B Place the letters below in **a b c** order.

1 n p o l m

2 v y w u x

3 q r u t v s

4 d f b a e c

5 i k h g f j

The Hall family

Use the words in the list on the left to fill the gaps in these sentences.

ball
banana
book
cat
family
fire
five
floor
girl
hands
letter
mother
television

1 This is the Hall ____ .

2 There are ____ people in all.

3 The father is reading a ____ .

4 He is also eating a ____ .

5 The ____ is writing a ____ .

6 The baby is sitting on the ____ .

7 He has a ____ in his ____ .

8 The ____ is playing with the ____ .

9 The dog is asleep by the ____ .

10 The boy is watching the ____ .

Doing words

When we add **-ing** to some doing words we **double the last letter**.

bat	batting
chop	chopping
clap	clapping
cut	cutting
run	running
sit	sitting
skip	skipping
swim	swimming

A Make a list of the doing words which fit these pictures.
Number them from 1 to 8.

B Fill the gap in each sentence by adding **-ing** to the word in bold type at the end of each line.

1 Andy kept ____ on the ice. **slip**

2 Chris enjoyed ____ the garden. **dig**

3 The bus will be ____ at the school gates. **stop**

4 We shall be ____ off there. **get**

5 The leaves lay ____ on the ground. **rot**

6 I am ____ my toys away. **put**

7 Roy went out without ____ the door. **shut**

8 Carol was ____ a new sweater. **knit**

Capital letters

This girl's name is Sally Ann Field.

The name of her pet cat is Skipper.

The girl's last name, **Field**, is her **surname**.

Her other names, **Sally Ann**, are her **Christian names** or **first names**.

The names of people and pets always begin with a **capital letter**.

The word **I** is always a capital letter.

What shall **I** have to eat?

A   Write your first names and your surname.

Now write out these sentences, using capital letters for the names of people and pets.

1   I told mary that I would play with her after tea.

2   When peggy fell down paul helped her up.

3   I think david maggs is taller than john perry.

4   The names of the twins are pamela and kenneth.

5   I saw roy bond feeding his dog sam.

6   We saw daisy the cow being milked.

7   linda named her new pony sunshine.

8   The name of our cat is fluffy.

B   Write a capital **I** in each space.

1   Where did ____ put my comb?

2   Do you think ____ am tall for my age?

3   Marion said ____ could have an orange.

4   ____ think ____ have a cold coming on.

5   When ____ am tired ____ lie down and rest.

Names and initials

Mr. Brown   Mrs. Brown   Miss James   Dr. Baker

The name of Joan's father is Mr. Norman Brown.

Her mother's name is Mrs. June Brown.

The name of Joan's teacher is **Miss** Freda James.

The family doctor is Dr. John Baker.

Instead of writing a person's first name, we sometimes write only the first letter.

For **Richard** we write **R**.

For **Mary** we write **M**.

We call these letters **initials**.

initials are always followed by **full stop**.

Mr. is a short way of writing **Mister**.

Mrs. is a short way of writing **Mistress**.

There is no short way of writing **Miss**.

Dr. is a short way of writing **Doctor**.

Write these names the short way, using initials for the first names.

A
1 Mister John Cobb
2 Mister Henry Watts
3 Mister David Roy Bond

B
1 Mistress Irene Bevan
2 Mistress Doreen Gaye
3 Mistress Joy Ann Davis

C
1 Miss Jennifer Mason
2 Miss Dorothy Eynon
3 Miss Anna May Carr

D
1 Doctor William Penn
2 Doctor Howard Taylor
3 Doctor Mark Ian Fox

Numbers the teens

one and ten = **eleven**	**11**
two and ten = **twelve** (dozen)	**12**
three and ten = **thirteen**	**13**
four and ten = **fourteen**	**14**
five and ten = **fifteen**	**15**
six and ten = **sixteen**	**16**
seven and ten = **seventeen**	**17**
eight and ten = **eighteen**	**18**
nine and ten = **nineteen**	**19**

teen means **and ten**

1   Which word means three and ten?

2   Dozen is another name for ____ .

3   ____ is one less than twelve.

4   The last teen number is ____ .

5   The number ____ is seven more than ten.

6   William is fourteen years old.
    He will be ____ next birthday.

7   Sheila had ten red beads and four blue ones.
    She had ____ altogether.

8   After Eric had lost one of his nineteen marbles
    he had ____ left.

9   ____ is twice as big as six.

10 Write the word for 16.

11 Write the words for the four even numbers.

12 Write the words for the five odd numbers.

More than one

one chick   two chick**s**

one bear   three bear**s**

A Write the missing words.

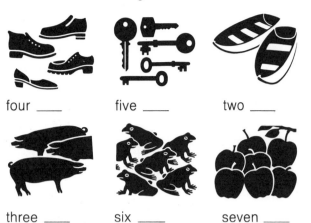

four _____   five _____   two _____

three _____   six _____   seven _____

B Copy these naming words.
Write **s** after each to make it mean **more than one**.

1	hen	5	duck	9	nut
2	cow	6	horse	10	sweet
3	ship	7	boat	11	cap
4	pen	8	sock	12	shoe

C What are the missing words?

1 one dog   four _____

2 one leg   two _____

3 one girl   five _____

4 one week   three _____

5 one day   six _____

6 a sweet   a bag of _____

7 a chocolate   a box of _____

8 a card   a pack of _____

9 a book   many _____

10 a boy   a few _____

Verses

Read the verses. Then do the exercises.

A   The Alchemist

There lives an old man at the top of the street,
And the end of his beard reaches down to his feet,
And he's just the one person I'm longing to meet,
I think that he sounds so exciting;
For he talks all the day to his tortoiseshell cat,
And he asks about this and explains about that,
And at night he puts on a big wide-awake* hat
And sits in the writing-room, writing.

*So as not to go to sleep

A. A. Milne

1 The _____ lives at the _____ of the street.

2 All day long he _____ to his cat.

3 At night he puts on a ___ ___ ___ ___ .

4 The old man's _____ reaches to his _____ .

B   The Vulture

The vulture eats between his meals,
And that's the reason why
He very, very rarely feels
As well as you or I.

His eye is dull, his head is bald,
His neck is growing thinner.
Oh! What a lesson for us all
To only eat at dinner!

Hilaire Belloc

1 The vulture's _____ is growing thinner.

2 His eye is _____ and his _____ is bald.

3 He rarely feels as _____ as you or _____ .

4 This is because he _____ between _____ .

He and she

A **boy** is a **he**.   A **girl** is a **she**.

He	She
boy	girl
brother	sister
father	mother
husband	wife
king	queen
lord	lady
man	woman
nephew	niece
prince	princess
uncle	aunt

A   Learn the words in the list on the left, then write the words which are missing from each sentence.

1   Lord and ____ Thompson opened the village fête.

2   James spent a holiday with his uncle and ____ .

3   There is work to do for every man and ____ .

4   Tony took his ____ and niece to the museum.

5   Both husband and ____ played tennis badly.

6   The king and ____ ruled for many years.

7   Bob and Pam are brother and ____ .

8   Bob is a lazy boy. Pam is a grumpy ____ .

B   Give the missing words.

1   ____ and wife   5   ____ and sister

2   ____ and lady   6   ____ and princess

3   ____ and aunt   7   ____ and mother

4   ____ and niece   8   ____ and queen

Days of the week

1 Sunday

2 Monday

3 Tuesday

4 Wednesday

5 Thursday

6 Friday

7 Saturday

The name of every day of the week begins with a **capital letter**.

Learn the names of the days and the order in which they come.

Solomon Grundy

Solomon Grundy,
Born on a Monday,
Christened on Tuesday,
Married on Wednesday,
Took ill on Thursday,
Worse on Friday,
Died on Saturday,
Buried on Sunday
That was the end of
Solomon Grundy.

Write the name of the day which will fill each gap in these sentences.

1 If today is Wednesday, yesterday was ____ .

2 Which day of the week has most letters in its name?

3 The school is closed on ____ and ____ .

4 ____ comes between Wednesday and Friday.

5 The day before Thursday is ____ .

6 Solomon Grundy was born on a ____ .

7 On ____ many people go to church.

8 If today is Friday, then tomorrow will be ____ .

9 Which day has in its name a letter **d** which is silent?

10 Sunday is the first day of the week. Which is the last day?

More than one

one box   two box**es**

We add **-es** to box to show
more than one.

one bus   three bus**es**

We add **-es** to bus to show
more than one.

A Write the missing words.
Each ends with **-es**.

1 one bush   four ____

2 one watch   six ____

3 one coach   two ____

4 one brush   five ____

5 one box   nine ____

6 one peach   a dish of ____

7 a dish   a set of ____

8 a church   a few ____

9 a torch   many ____

10 a match   a box of ____

B Use the words you have made to fill these
gaps.

1 The jeweller sold many different clocks
and ____ .

2 There were lots of gooseberries on the ____ .

3 Many ____ have a tall tower.

4 Janet dropped the ____ on the floor.

5 The man used four ____ to light the fire.

6 Two ____ took the party to town.

7 Alan got the ____ to clean his shoes.

8 Emma was given two ____ of chocolates.

9 Adrian bought a tin of ____ and a tin of cream.

10 Some ____ throw their light a long way.

Capital letters

Look at this address.

The **name of the street** begins with a **capital letter**.

The **name of the town** begins with a **capital letter**.

The **name of the county**, Sussex, and the postcode have **capital letters**.

The names of places always begin with a **capital letter**.

Miss Ann Page,
24 Main Street,
Brighton,
East Sussex BR1 3HS

A Write these sentences, using capital letters for the names of all places. End each sentence with a full stop.

1 london is the capital of england

2 Ships sail from dover

3 He was born in oxford

4 bath is a very old city

5 Jane lives in ashton road, bristol

6 We went by train to york

7 The liner docked in liverpool

8 The biggest city in wales is cardiff

9 many people visit windsor castle

10 He has moved from station road to oak avenue

B

1 Write your own name and address.

2 Write the name and address of any friend.

3 Write the name and address of any relation.

To, two and too

To, **two** and **too** all have a similar sound.

Going **to** bed

Going **to** sleep

The **two** pigs

Each has **two** ears

He is **too** old to work.
(more than enough)

He is very bent, **too**.
(also)

To, **two** and **too** have different meanings.

Write **to**, **two** or **too** in each space below.

1 Alan went ＿＿ bed early.

2 ＿＿ and ＿＿ make four.

3 He is ＿＿ ill ＿＿ go ＿＿ school.

4 It is nearly ＿＿ o'clock.

5 Are you going ＿＿ help me?

6 I am going ＿＿ sit down in the shade.

7 It is ＿＿ hot ＿＿ play games.

8 The ＿＿ girls were great friends.

9 Are you coming ＿＿ London, ＿＿ ?

10 Jim is getting ＿＿ fat ＿＿ walk.

Busy children

boys
easel
five
front
girls
house
jar

looking
painting
pencils
picture
rabbit
showing
table

Look at the picture carefully.
Use the words in the list on the left to fill the gaps.

1 There are ___ children in the picture.

2 Two of them are ___ and three are ___ .

3 Roger has made a ___ out of clay.

4 Susan has done a drawing and is ___ it to ___ .

5 There is a ___ of water in ___ of Alan.

6 Mary is ___ a ___ of a house.

7 Her picture is standing on the ___ .

8 Ann has a set of coloured ___ .

9 ___ sits at the end of the ___ .

10 ___ is the only child standing.

Alan   Susan   Roger   Mary   Ann

24

Numbers the tens

20 **twenty** means **two tens**

30 **thirty** means **three tens**

40 **forty** means **four tens**

50 **fifty** means **five tens**

60 **sixty** means **six tens**

70 **seventy** means **seven tens**

80 **eighty** means **eight tens**

90 **ninety** means **nine tens**

100 **hundred** means **ten tens**

A   Write the words which fill the gaps.

1 Seven tens are ____ .

2 The number ____ is one half of a hundred.

3 Four times ten are ____ .

4 Six rows of ten make ____ .

5 Three tens are ____ .

When we write a **units** word after a **tens** word we use a hyphen -.

six tens and four units
sixty and four
sixty-four

B   Write the words for –

a 42

b 97

c 78

d 54

e 83

f two tens and nine units

g nine tens and four units

h eight tens and five units

i three tens and eight units

Colours

Look at the list of colours below.

Learn how to spell each word, then answer the questions.

black
blue
brown
green
grey
red
white
yellow

A What is the colour of:

1 a buttercup   6 a postbox

2 grass   7 a ripe banana

3 tar   8 a snowdrop

4 a ruby   9 a ripe tomato

5 chocolate   10 a polar bear

B Write the name of anything which is:

1 black

2 white

3 red

4 green

5 yellow

C Write these sentences, putting in the missing words.

1 In spring the leaves on the trees are ____ .

2 When the traffic light is ____ the traffic must stop.

3 When the traffic light is ____ the traffic can go.

4 Butter is ____ in colour.

5 The roofs of the houses were ____ with snow.

6 A policeman wears a dark ____ uniform.

7 A lump of coal is ____ in colour.

8 When bread is toasted it turns ____ .

9 The robin has a ____ breast.

10 When people get old their hair turns ____ or ____ .

More than one

one pon**y**   two pon**ies**

one dais**y**   four dais**ies**

To make the words **pony** and **daisy** mean **more than one** we change the **y** to **i** before adding **-es**.

pony	daisy
poni	daisi
ponies	daisies

A   Now do the same with these words which end with **y**.

1   fly   a swarm of ____

2   pony   two ____

3   puppy   a litter of ____

4   berry   a cluster of ____

5   daisy   a chain of ____

6   gipsy   several ____

7   story   a book of ____

8   fairy   many ____

9   baby   four ____

10 lady   a few ____

B   Use the words you have made to fill these gaps.

1   Holly ____ are red when they are ripe.

2   Young ____ are fed on milk.

3   Our corgi had four ____ today.

4   Three ____ were grazing in the field.

5   David likes to read ____ about animals.

6   The ____ live in caravans on the moor.

7   Several ____ were buzzing round the jam.

8   Do you believe in ____ ?

More than one

one loa**f**   two loa**ves**

one lea**f**   three lea**ves**

To make the words **loaf** and **leaf** mean **more than one**, we change the **f** to **v** before adding **-es**.

loaf   leaf
loav   leav
loaves   leaves

A   Now do the same with these words.

1 thief   ten ____
2 shelf   three ____
3 loaf   five ____
4 half   two ____
5 calf   four ____
6 leaf   many ____
7 sheaf   ten ____
8 wolf   a pack of ____

With these words, change the **f** to **v** and add **-s**. The **e** is there already.

9   wife ____
10 life ____
11 knife ____

B   Use the words you have made to fill these gaps.

1 The ____ in the shop were full of toys.
2 The baker sold dozens of ____ of bread yesterday.
3 In autumn ____ fall from many trees.
4 There are two ____ in a whole one.
5 Baby cows are called ____ .
6 ____ are wild dogs.
7 The butcher has very sharp ____ .
8 The police caught the car ____ .

Adding -ed to doing words

To make a doing word show
past time we add **-ed**.

Now	Past
Today I play	Yesterday I play**ed**.
Today I work	Last week I work**ed**.

A Add **-ed** to each of these doing words.

1 rain   6 bark

2 play   7 fill

3 chew   8 pick

4 wait   9 open

5 ask   10 fetch

B Use the words you have made to fill
the gaps in these sentences.

1 Jane ____ her mother for another cake.

2 Simon ____ an apple off the tree.

3 The dog ____ at the postman.

4 Jill ____ the paper for her parents.

5 The kitten ____ with the ball.

6 The man ____ for an hour for the bus.

7 Terry ____ the bucket with water.

8 It ____ all day yesterday.

9 The cow ____ the grass for a long time.

10 He ____ the door and went in.

Martin's toys

Martin has a big cupboard full of toys. Some are new but most of them are old. He will not get rid of any of them.

The toy he likes best is his clockwork train. The oldest toy is a teddy bear. His mother bought it for his first birthday.

Martin also has a big crane and a tractor. These are almost new. The crane can lift the tractor right off the floor.

1 Martin keeps his toys in a big ____ .

2 ____ of them are new but ____ of them are ____ .

3 Martin likes his ____ ____ best of all.

4 The ____ toy is a teddy bear.

5 Martin had it when he was a ____ old.

6 His ____ bought it for him.

7 The ____ was a birthday present from his ____

8 The ____ can lift the ____ right off the ____ .

Using is and are/Using was and were

The tree **is** bare.
We use **is** for **one** tree.

The trees **are** bare.
We use **are** for **more than one**.

We use **was** for one person or thing.

We use **were** for more than one person or thing.

A   Fill each space with **is** or **are**.

1   This apple ____ sour.
     These apples ____ sour.

2   ____ the house old?
     ____ the houses old?

3   The dog ____ barking.
     The dogs ____ barking.

4   ____ the egg fresh?
     ____ the eggs fresh?

B   Fill each space with **was** or **were**.

1   One egg ____ cracked.
     Three eggs ____ cracked.

2   The girl ____ skipping.
     The girls ____ skipping.

3   ____ the orange sweet?
     ____ the oranges sweet?

4   The cow ____ being milked.
     The cows ____ being milked.

C   Choose the right word from the pair above to fill each space.

1   **is   are**
     Barbara ____ ill, but Anna ____ well.

2   **was   were**
     The hens ____ laying, so the farmer ____ pleased.

3   **was   were**
     The wind ____ cold and snow ____ falling.

4   **is   are**
     School ____ over and we ____ going home.

5   **was   were**
     They ____ glad because the day ____ sunny.

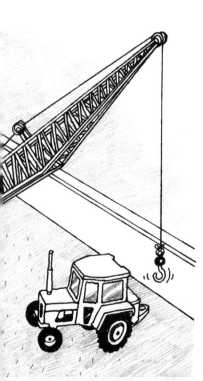

The alphabet

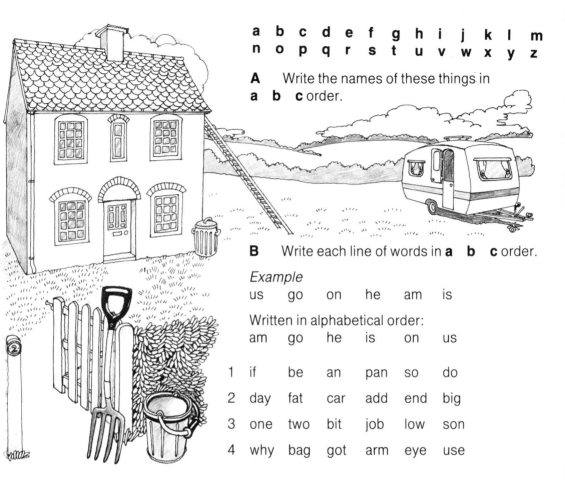

a b c d e f g h i j k l m
n o p q r s t u v w x y z

A   Write the names of these things in
a   b   c order.

B   Write each line of words in **a   b   c** order.

Example
us   go   on   he   am   is

Written in alphabetical order:
am   go   he   is   on   us

1   if   be   an   pan   so   do

2   day   fat   car   add   end   big

3   one   two   bit   job   low   son

4   why   bag   got   arm   eye   use

C   In each group below all the words are in
a   b   c order except one. Can you spot the
odd word?

In group 1 below the odd word is **gun**

1	arm	2	hat	3	bed	4	fat	5	queen
	ball		zoo		ear		goat		ring
	can		jar		kid		hut		bell
	deer		log		net		wet		tray
	gun		man		pad		ink		use
	egg		peg		cow		jug		van
	fan		rat		sun		king		web

Doing words   past time

To make a doing word show
past time we add **-ed**.

	Now	Past
	Today I play	Yesterday I play**ed**.
	Today I work	Last week I work**ed**.

But if the doing word ends with
e, we just add **-d**.

The snails move slowly.   The snails move**d** slowly.

A   Make each of these doing words show
past time by adding **-d**.

1	sneeze	5	hope	9	save
2	like	6	wave	10	joke
3	wipe	7	use	11	bake
4	fire	8	dive	12	move

B   Make the word to fill each space by adding
-d to the word in bold type.

1 Peter ____ loudly.   **sneeze**

2 They ____ to London last week.   **move**

3 The Queen ____ to the crowd.   **wave**

4 The farmer ____ his gun at the rooks.   **fire**

5 The sailor ____ into the rough sea.   **dive**

6 I ____ all the sugar to make some
cakes.   **use**

7 I have ____ fifty pence this week.   **save**

8 Helen ____ having sausages for lunch.   **like**

9 Ann ____ the baby's mouth.   **wipe**

10 The motorist ____ with the policeman.   **joke**

Adding -ed to doing words

When we add **-ed** to some
doing words we **double the
last letter**.

	rob	tug
Double the last letter.	rob**b**	tug**g**
Add on **-ed**.	rob**bed**	tug**ged**

A   Add **-ed** to each of these doing words.
Remember to double the last letter.

1	pin	6	hug
2	clap	7	wag
3	stop	8	chop
4	beg	9	hum
5	tap	10	sip

B   Use the words you have made to fill the
gaps in these sentences.

1   The little dog ____ for a bone.

2   He ____ his tail when he got it.

3   Betty ____ the hot tea slowly.

4   The bus ____ outside the school.

5   Jane ____ her new teddy bear.

6   Alan ____ at the door before going in.

7   Carol ____ a badge on to her jacket.

8   The scouts ____ the wood for the fire.

9   The children ____ their hands for joy.

10   A swarm of bees ____ round our heads.

Putting sentences in order

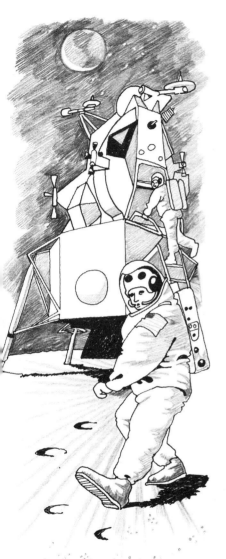

Here are four short stories.
The sentences in them are in the wrong order.
Write them as they should be.

1 a He paid the shopkeeper.

   b He joined his friends outside.

   c James went into the sweet shop.

   d He put the change in his pocket.

   e He asked for a packet of mints.

2 a She drank all the milk.

   b She put a straw in the bottle.

   c She put the empty bottle in the crate.

   d Wendy took a bottle of milk from the crate.

   e She took off the cap.

3 a He went to the bathroom to wash himself.

   b He went off to catch the school bus.

   c He ate his breakfast and left the table.

   d He dressed himself and went downstairs.

   e Michael got out of bed at eight o'clock.

4 a They walked about collecting moon rocks.

   b The rocket took off from the moon with a loud blast from its engines.

   c Two spacemen climbed out of the rocket.

   d The rocket landed safely on the moon.

   e The spacemen climbed back into their rocket.

Going to school

John Dawes and his sister Ann go to the same school. John is two years older than Ann. He is in Class 3 and Ann is in Class 1.

The school is quite near their home and so they walk there each day. Before breakfast John takes his dog, Bobby, for a long walk and Ann feeds her two rabbits, Snowy and Sooty.

John and Ann often meet their friends on the way to school and they always say hallo to Mrs Davies the lollipop lady.

1 What is the name of Ann's brother?

2 Do John and Ann go to the same school?

3 In what class is Ann?

4 Do they live near the school or far from it?

5 What does John do every morning before school?

6 What does his sister do?

7 What colours are Ann's rabbits?

8 Who is Mrs Davies and what does she do?

Opposites using un

tidy

untidy

We can give some words an opposite meaning by writing **un** before them.

Look at the words below the pictures.

A Write the opposites of these words by using **un**.

1	lock	5	kind	9	known
2	paid	6	do	10	tie
3	well	7	screw	11	load
4	pack	8	wind	12	wrap

B Choose any six of the words you have made and use them in sentences of your own.

C Write out these sentences, adding **un** to the words in bold type so as to give them an opposite meaning.

1 It did not take Susan long to **dress**.

2 The room was very **tidy**.

3 This water is **fit** for drinking.

4 What he said was **true**.

5 The injured man was **able** to walk.

6 Tom sat in a corner looking very **happy**.

7 They were **willing** to go.

8 The bridge was **safe** for traffic.

Opposites change of words

tall

short

The words **tall** and **short** are **opposite** in meaning.

bad	good
big	small
cold	hot
early	late
empty	full
hard	soft
in	out
new	old
open	shut
strong	weak
tall	short
tame	wild

Learn the pairs of opposites in the list on the left, then put the right word in each space in the sentences below.

1 Barry bought a new car and sold the ____ one.

2 We had a ____ day out even though the weather was bad.

3 I was late for school yesterday, but I was ____ today.

4 The lion is strong, but the mouse is ____ .

5 There was hot and ____ water in the bathroom.

6 Some apples are hard; others are ____ .

7 Mr. Wells was in, but Mrs. Wells was ____ .

8 Paul is a tall boy, but his brother Mark is quite ____ .

9 The shop is open on Saturday and ____ on Sunday.

10 Some horses are wild and some are ____ .

Adding -ed to doing words

When we add **-ed** to doing words ending with **y** we change the **y** to **i**.

	try	marry
Change the **y** to **i**	tr**i**	marr**i**
Add on **-ed**	tr**ied**	marr**ied**

With these words the **y** is changed to **i** and **-d** only is added.

pay	lay	say
paid	laid	said

I tidy my bedroom

I tidied my bedroom

A Add **-ed** to each of these words. Remember to change the **y** to **i**.

1 dry	4 tidy	7 hurry
2 carry	5 cry	8 fry
3 copy	6 bury	9 empty

B Use the words you have learnt to fill the spaces.

1 I ___ to catch the train.

2 We had ___ bacon and eggs for breakfast.

3 Janet ___ when she fell off the wall.

4 Keith ___ the heavy basket all the way home.

5 The sun and the wind soon ___ the washing.

6 Robert ___ the room after the party.

7 The dog ___ a bone in the garden.

8 Bill ___ the words in his notebook.

9 I ___ the butcher for the meat.

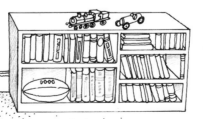

Two word games

A   By writing letter **s** before **pill** we make the word **spill**.

Write a letter before each word in bold type to make the word which fills the gap.

1   She wore ____ trousers at the party.   **ink**

2   The plate was too hot to ____ .   **old**

3   We watched the top ____ round and round.   **pin**

4   We ____ to read at school.   **earn**

5   The ____ of the ticket was fifty pence.   **rice**

6   The children made a sandcastle on the ____ .   **each**

7   Susan used a ____ to sweep the path.   **room**

8   An animal is sometimes called a ____ .   **east**

B   From the letters in the word **rats** we can make the word **star**.

From the letters in the words in bold type make words which will fit into the spaces.

1   He could not ____ the heavy chest.   **flit**

2   Jean had a bruise on her ____ .   **inch**

3   The wind had blown every ____ off the tree.   **flea**

4   Philip came second in the sack ____ .   **care**

5   The oranges were ten pence ____ .   **ache**

6   Colin clapped and cheered when his ____ won the cup.   **tame**

7   Anne was the ____ to go to bed.   **salt**

8   The children jumped ____ the stream.   **rove**

Using is and his / Using as and has

It **is** cold.
Sally **is** ill.

Is and **are** are partners.

Hugh lost **his** book.
His means **belonging to him**.

His and **her** are partners.

As I turned I slipped.
It was **as** cold **as** ice.

Bob **has** a football.
Has means **owns**.

Bob **has** a football.
    owns

A   Use **is** or **his** to fill each space.

1   This book ____ really funny.

2   Father cut ____ finger with a sharp knife.

3   Billy often gives ____ dog a bone.

4   The dog ____ a fox terrier.

5   ____ uncle ____ a farmer.

6   When ____ Roy going to eat ____ apple?

7   Ann ____ seven, but David ____ only five.

8   Alan helps both ____ father and ____ mother.

B   Use **as** or **has** to fill each space.

1   Richard ____ a new bat.

2   June is ____ tall ____ Helen.

3   He whistled ____ he worked.

4   Where ____ Karen put the sweets?

5   He knocked his head ____ he bent down.

6   ____ anybody seen my book?

7   I think Linda ____ grown ____ tall ____ Jane.

8   Father ____ a bath ____ soon ____ he comes home.

Little Robin Redbreast

Little Robin Redbreast
  Sat upon a tree,
He sang merrily,
  As merrily as could be.
He nodded with his head,
  And his tail waggled he,
As little Robin Redbreast
  Sat upon a tree.

Welcome little Robin
  With your scarlet breast,
In this winter weather
  Cold must be your nest.
Hopping on the carpet,
  Picking up the crumbs,
Robin knows the children
  Love him when he comes.

Copy the sentences.
Fill the spaces.

1 Robin sat upon a ＿＿ .

2 Robin ＿＿ as merrily as could be.

3 He ＿＿ with his head.

4 He waggled his ＿＿ .

5 Robin has a scarlet ＿＿ .

6 In the ＿＿ his nest is ＿＿ .

7 Robin hops on the ＿＿ and picks up the ＿＿ .

8 Robin knows the ＿＿ love him when he ＿＿ .

Roger and Pam

This is Roger.   This is Pam.

A   See how Roger is dressed.
Use the words in the list on the left to fill the spaces.

jeans
shoes
anorak
bobble-hat
sweater

1   On his head Roger wears a ＿＿ .

2   His ＿＿ keeps the wind out.

3   On his feet he wears blue ＿＿ .

4   Under his anorak he wears a ＿＿ .

5   Roger wears a belt to keep his ＿＿ up.

B   See what Pam is wearing. Use the words in the list on the left to fill the spaces.

jacket
scarf
skirt
boots
gloves

1   Pam wears a check ＿＿ .

2   Round her neck she wears a long woolly ＿＿ .

3   On her feet she wears blue ＿＿ .

4   She wears a blue pleated ＿＿ .

5   Pam wears ＿＿ to keep her hands warm.

Write a few sentences telling how any boy or girl in your class is dressed.

Things we eat and drink

Our milkman brings us a **bottle** of milk every day.

We can buy a **loaf** of bread from the baker.

Copy the words below and fill in the gaps. The words you need are in exercise B.

A

1   a bunch of ___   2   a bar of ___   3   a tin of ___   4   a bottle of ___

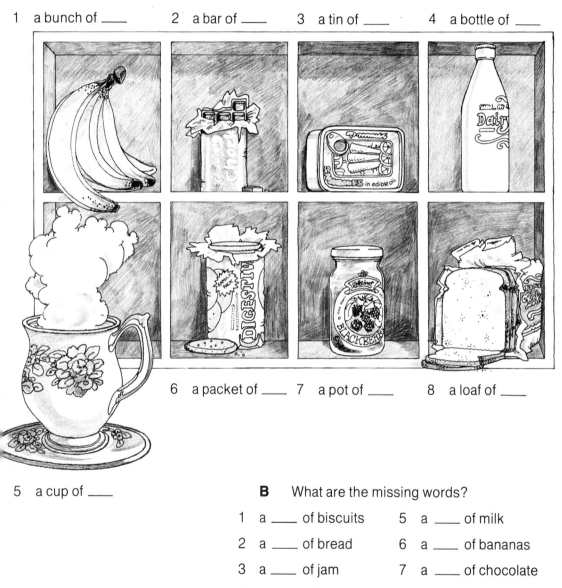

6   a packet of ___   7   a pot of ___   8   a loaf of ___

5   a cup of ___

B   What are the missing words?

1   a ___ of biscuits   5   a ___ of milk

2   a ___ of bread   6   a ___ of bananas

3   a ___ of jam   7   a ___ of chocolate

4   a ___ of tea   8   a ___ of sardines

Rhymes

Pussy Cat, Pussy Cat, where have you been?
I've been to London to look at the Queen.
Pussy Cat, Pussy Cat, what did you there?
I frightened a little mouse under the chair.

The words **been** and **Queen** end with the same sound.

So do the words **there** and **chair**.

Words which end with the same sound are said to **rhyme**.

A   Write the two words that rhyme in each group below.

1	man	2	bed	3	same
	far		bee		take
	bat		leg		tale
	can		pen		pane
	tap		pet		sail
	wag		sea		race

4	team	5	fear	6	late
	seat		beat		laid
	lean		bear		wait
	leap		hail		pain
	seed		hair		sail
	meet		real		page

B   Here are twenty words. Write them as ten pairs of words which rhyme, like this:

trip   sore   mill
ship   four   fill

1	trip	8	peas	15	seal
2	sore	9	pull	16	card
3	mill	10	hard	17	full
4	down	11	brown	18	fill
5	line	12	fine	19	bees
6	peel	13	ship	20	harm
7	four	14	farm		

Using has and have

For **one** person or thing we use **has**.

For **more than one** person or thing we use **have**.

Always use **have** with **I** or **you**.

Our cat **has** kittens.
Uncle Ben **has** bought a new car.

The monkeys **have** long tails.
The children **have** gone to the circus.

I **have** a bad cold.
You **have** grown quite a lot.

A   Write **has** or **have** in each space.

1   Simon ____ lost his dinner money.

2   Where ____ you been all day?

3   The books ____ been left out.

4   The book ____ been left out.

5   ____ father come home yet?

6   ____ the children come home yet?

7   Both the kittens ____ grey fur.

8   ____ the postman called?

9   The elephant ____ a long trunk.

10 Elephants ____ long trunks.

B   Write three sentences of your own using **has**, and three using **have**.

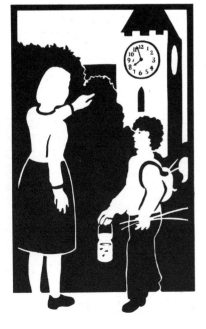

46

Words with more than one meaning

Some words have more than one meaning.

Mind you do not **drop** that plate.

There is not a **drop** of milk left.

back
band
calf
lean
left
mine
post
stick
suit

Use the words in the list on the left to fill these spaces. The same word must be used for each pair of sentences.

1   My ___ is bad after weeding the garden.
    I will be ___ in half an hour.

2   A ___ is a young cow.
    The back of the leg below the knee is called the ___ .

3   A new ___ was put up to hold the clothes line.
    Would you like me to ___ your letter?

4   Please don't ___ against the glass door.
    This beef is very ___ .

5   Coal is dug out of a ___ .
    Your bat is much better than ___ .

6   The ___ played a lively tune.
    Jill had a wide ___ of ribbon round her hair.

7   George writes with his ___ hand.
    There are only two pears ___ in the dish.

8   Will you ___ a stamp on this envelope?
    He used a short ___ to make a fishing rod.

9   Brian wore his new blue ___ to the wedding.
    Maureen's new dress does not ___ her at all.

In the woods

Carol and her little sister Mary went for a walk in the woods one day. They took their dog Sammy with them. Sammy ran on in front of them. He knew the way very well, for he had been there many times before.

The children found some bluebells growing in the woods, so they picked a bunch for their mother. While they were doing this, Sammy saw a rabbit sitting under a tree. He barked loudly and ran after it. But he did not catch it, for the rabbit ran into a hole in the ground.

1 Carol and Mary ____ for a ____ in the ____ one day.

2 They ____ their dog ____ with ____ .

3 Sammy ____ on in front of ____ .

4 Sammy ____ the way.
  He had ____ there ____ times ____ .

5 The children ____ some ____ growing.

6 They ____ a ____ for their ____ .

7 Sammy saw a ____ sitting ____ a ____ .

8 He ran ____ it but did not ____ it.

Same sound — different meaning

Some words have the same sound as other words, but they are different in spelling and in meaning.

Look at these four pairs of words.

one   You have **one** nose and one mouth.

won   Jack **won** a prize for good writing.

by   He was standing **by** the door.

buy   I will **buy** you a bar of chocolate.

made The toy was **made** in England.

maid The **maid** dusted the chairs.

tale A **tale** is a story.

tail The squirrel has a bushy **tail**.

Choose the right word from the pair above to fill each space.

1 **one   won**
  Wilson ____ the race easily.

2 **tale   tail**
  Paul read a fairy ____ to Janet.

3 **by   buy**
  I am going to ____ some sweets.

4 **one   won**
  There was only ____ apple left.

5 **made   maid**
  Penny ____ a dress for herself.

6 **tale   tail**
  Our dog wags his ____ when he is happy.

7 **by   buy**
  The family went to London ____ train.

8 **made   maid**
  The new ____ tidied the bedrooms in the hotel.

People who work

A Use the words in the list to name each person. Number your words from 1 to 8 as in the pictures.

baker   milkman
butcher   miner
doctor   pilot
dustman   postman
farmer   zoo keeper
grocer

B Who am I?

1   I bring letters and parcels to your home.

2   You buy meat from me.

3   I try to cure you when you are ill.

4   I bring milk to your home every day.

5   I dig coal from the earth.

6   I look after lots of different animals.

7   I fly aeroplanes all over the world.

8   I make bread, buns and cakes.

9   I collect rubbish from your house.

10   I sell bacon, cheese, jam, tea, sugar and other things.

The not words

We sometimes join **not** to another word.

When we do this we leave out the **o** in **not** and write **'** in its place.

Examples

is not	isn't
was not	wasn't
does not	doesn't
has not	hasn't
are not	aren't
were not	weren't
do not	don't
have not	haven't

Remember that the **'** must go where the **o** was.

A   Join each pair of words together.

1 does not
2 were not
3 has not
4 is not
5 have not
6 was not
7 do not
8 are not

B   Write these sentences, using one word in place of the two words in bold type in each line.

1 The cuckoo **does not** make a nest of its own.
2 The twins **were not** in school today.
3 Father **has not** gone to work yet.
4 This milk **is not** fresh.
5 **Was not** that a dainty dish to set before the king?
6 Some children **do not** have dinner at school.
7 We **have not** had the treat we were promised.
8 These oranges **are not** very sweet.

Using do and does

We use **does** when we speak of **one person or thing**.

We use **do** when we speak of **more than one**.

Always use **do** with **you**, even for one person.

Always use **do** with **I**.

One	More than one
I do	we do
you do	you do
he, she, it does	they do

A   Fill each space with **do** or **does**.

1   Martin ＿＿ his exercises every morning.

2   Many people ＿＿ exercises to keep fit.

3   I hope you ＿＿ well in the test.

4   Our dog ＿＿ like a meaty bone.

5   Susan and I ＿＿ our homework together.

6   Henry ＿＿ his best to keep the garden tidy.

B   **Don't** and **doesn't** follow the same rules.

Write **don't** or **doesn't** in each space.

1   We ＿＿ go to bed very early in summer.

2   The shop ＿＿ close till six o'clock.

3   Jane ＿＿ like washing up.

4   You will miss the bus if you ＿＿ hurry.

5   I ＿＿ go to the pictures very often.

6   Colin ＿＿ want any breakfast this morning.

Capital letters

Capital letters are used –

1 to begin a sentence

2 for the names of people and pets

3 for the names of places, rivers, mountains and so on

4 for the names of the days of the week and months of the year

A There are **fourteen words** in this list which should begin with a capital letter. Write them in the order in.which they come.

fine	france	monday
london	shoes	england
plate	nelson	jones
george	thames	table
bread	banana	arthur
friday	betty	chest
thomson	april	paper
apple	chicken	july

B Write these sentences in your book. Use **capital letters** where they are needed.

1 did you know that i was seven last sunday?

2 linda and charles live in church street.

3 roy goes to brighton every saturday.

4 i take my dog chum for a walk every day.

5 jack and jill went up the hill.

6 farmer grey has a cow named daisy.

7 we shall be moving to bristol next tuesday.

8 the severn is the longest river in england.

Children at play

Betty   Ann   David   Jill

James   Roger

Look at these children at play. Use the words from the list on the left to finish each sentence below.

branch
fast
holding
marbles
ring
skates
skipping
stick
swing
thick

1   David is on roller ___ .

2   He is going very ___ .

3   Betty and Ann are having a ___ race.

4   Roger and James are playing ___ .

5   James is ___ a marble in his right hand.

6   Jill is on the ___ .

7   The swing hangs from a ___ of the tree.

8   The trunk of the tree is very ___ .

Joining words

Some words are made by joining two words together.

arm + chair = armchair

A   The names of things you see in the pictures are made in this way. Copy them from the list on the left.

birdcage   snowman
cupboard   tablecloth
eggcup   teapot
flowerpot   wallpaper

B   Join the two words in bold type in each phrase to make one word, starting with the second word.

Example   1   milkman

1   The **man** who brings **milk** to your home

2   A **mill** which is worked by the **wind**

3   The land at the **side** of the **sea**

4   A **bin** in which **dust** is put

5   A **band** of ribbon for a **hat**

6   A **bag** carried in the **hand**

7   The **sty** in which a **pig** is kept

8   A **room** for a **bed**

9   A **ball** game which is played with the **foot**

10   The **bell** on a **door**

Doing words past time

We do not always add **-ed** to doing words to show **past time**.

	Now	Past
	Today I **fly**.	Yesterday I **flew**.
	Today I **come**.	Last week I **came**.

Learn the words in the list, then do the exercises.

Present	Past
bite	bit
break	broke
come	came
creep	crept
do	did
draw	drew
drink	drank
fall	fell
fly	flew
give	gave
hide	hid
wear	wore

A   Copy these columns. Fill the blanks.

Present Past

	Present	Past			Present	Past
1	draw	_____	7	_____	broke
2	drink	_____	8	_____	hid
3	bite	_____	9	_____	crept
4	fly	_____	10	do	_____
5	_____	came	11	_____	fell
6	_____	wore	12	give	_____

B   Put the right word in each space.

1 Ronald ____ the ball in the drawer.   **hide**

2 Mrs. Dobbs ____ Marion a cream bun.   **give**

3 The robin ____ away when we got near.   **fly**

4 A big dog ____ Susan on the leg.   **bite**

5 Who ____ this lovely picture?   **draw**

6 The football ____ the window.   **break**

7 Philip ____ his best writing.   **do**

8 Jill ____ her new shoes yesterday.   **wear**

Opposites change of word

Learn this list of opposites,
then answer the questions.

begin	finish
bottom	top
clean	dirty
down	up
dry	wet
fresh	stale
give	take
high	low
over	under
pretty	ugly
right	wrong
thick	thin

A   Write the opposites of these words.

1 ugly   7 down

2 thin   8 bottom

3 wrong   9 dirty

4 under   10 finish

5 stale   11 dry

6 take   12 high

B   Copy these sentences. In each space
write the opposite of the word in bold type.

1 Simon rode **up** the lane, then ＿＿ again.

2 The show will **begin** at 7 o'clock and ＿＿ at
9 o'clock.

3 The **clean** plates were put away and
the ＿＿ ones were put in the sink.

4 The ＿＿ of the pole was thicker than the **top**.

5 Three sums were **right** and one was ＿＿ .

6 The baker had no **fresh** loaves, only ＿＿ ones.

7 Please **take** this tea away and ＿＿ me some
milk.

8 Tim jumped **over** the bar. David ducked ＿＿ it.

9 Jeremy likes **thick** slices of bread. Jean only
eats ＿＿ slices.

10 Sally looks **pretty** when she smiles
but ＿＿ when she frowns.

Same sound — different meaning

Look at the four pairs of words below.

The words in each pair have the same sound but are different in spelling and meaning.

not	Mrs. Young was **not** at home.
knot	There was a **knot** in the rope.
new	The **new** car is faster than the old one.
knew	Richard **knew** all the songs the class sang.
sea	Several ships were sailing on the **sea**.
see	We **see** with our eyes.
our	**Our** things are the things that belong to us.
hour	There are sixty minutes in an **hour**.

Fill each space with the right word.

1 Henry wore his ___ blazer to school.

2 The boat was wrecked in the stormy ___ .

3 I did ___ eat the apple because it was bad.

4 Jenny ___ her tables well.

5 We put ___ books under the desks.

6 From the top of the tower we could ___ the ___ .

7 James could ___ untie the ___ in his shoelace.

8 The schoolchildren get an ___ for lunch.

58

Collections

Look at the words used for each collection below.

We call a number of sheep together a **flock**.

1   a box of ___

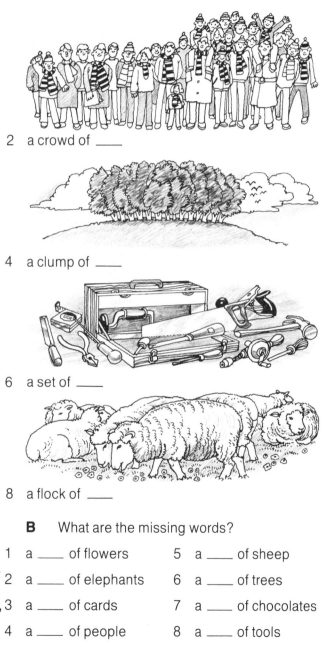

2   a crowd of ___

3   a bunch of ___

4   a clump of ___

5   a pack of ___

6   a set of ___

7   a herd of ___

8   a flock of ___

B   What are the missing words?

1   a ___ of flowers   5   a ___ of sheep

2   a ___ of elephants   6   a ___ of trees

3   a ___ of cards   7   a ___ of chocolates

4   a ___ of people   8   a ___ of tools

59

Sausages for supper

Every Saturday, Rachel has her favourite food for supper.

Her mother fries some fat, juicy sausages and a pile of crisp, golden chips. Rachel always clears her plate and usually has a second helping.

For pudding, Rachel has a large bowl of ice-cream, sometimes strawberry flavour, sometimes chocolate. Her mother gives her a wafer biscuit to go with it. Rachel breaks the wafer into quarters and sticks the pieces in her ice-cream to make a little sailing-boat.

Rachel wishes she could have her favourite food every day.

1 How often does Rachel have her favourite food?

2 How does Rachel's mother cook the sausages?

3 What colour are the chips?

4 How many helpings does Rachel usually have?

5 What is Rachel's pudding served in?

6 What are the two colours of Rachel's ice-cream?

7 How many pieces of wafer are there in her sailing-boat?

8 How often would Rachel like sausages and chips?

Showing ownership

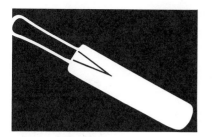

This is Ian's bat.

The **'s** shows that Ian **owns** the bat.

Look at these pictures.

See who **owns** each thing.

Write **'s** after each child's name to finish the exercise. The first is done for you.

1   Ian

2   Sarah

3   Ann

4   Peter

5   Alan

6   Janet

7   David

8   Pam

Copy these in your book.

1   Ian's bat

2   ____ teddy bear

3   ____ ball

4   ____ top

5   ____ car

6   ____ pram

7   ____ scooter

8   ____ cat

Groups

A pansy is a **flower**.   A cat is an **animal**.   A rook is a **bird**.   A fir is a **tree**.

A   Draw four columns in your book like these.
Then put the words below in their proper places.

Animals	Birds	Trees	Flowers
beech	thrush	oak	fir
robin	pig	cow	rose
tulip	daisy	lark	goat
sheep	rook	pansy	elm

B   Draw these four columns in your book.
Put the words in their proper places.

Tools	Clothes	Furniture	Colours
table	coat	yellow	axe
spanner	hammer	shorts	wardrobe
green	shirt	jersey	saw
chair	settee	blue	brown

Similars

Some words mean much the same as other words:

A **large** house
A **big** house

The words **large** and **big** are **similar**, or **alike**, in meaning.

Learn these similars, then do the exercises.

creep	crawl
finish	end
halt	stop
large	big
present	gift
speak	talk
start	begin
stout	fat
tear	rip
tug	pull

A   In place of each word in bold type write a word which has a **similar** meaning.

1   I **start** work at eight o'clock.

2   Snakes **creep** along the ground.

3   John gave Jane's hair a playful **tug**.

4   A **large** crowd saw a fine game.

5   They do not **speak** to each other now.

6   Cars must **halt** at the crossroads.

7   The cook was a **stout** person.

8   There is a **tear** in my coat.

9   Carol had a lovely **present** from her aunt.

10   Our holiday will **finish** next Sunday.

B   For each word below write one which is similar in meaning.

1   big

2   talk

3   end

4   pull

5   gift

6   crawl

7   stop

8   begin

Describing words

The rabbit has **long** ears.

The word **long** tells **what kind** of ears the rabbit has.

Because it **describes** the ears, we call it a **describing** word.

A   Choose one of the words in the list on the left to describe each of the things below.

fast
gold
tasty
kind
shady
sour
savage
silk
blazing
rough

1   a ____ dog   6   a ____ fire

2   a ____ tree   7   a ____ meal

3   a ____ sea   8   a ____ car

4   a ____ ring   9   a ____ friend

5   a ____ blouse   10   a ____ apple

B   Now use the best describing word you can think of for each of these words.

1   a ____ boy   5   a ____ field

2   a ____ wind   6   a ____ flower

3   a ____ dress   7   a ____ kitten

4   a ____ policeman   8   a ____ orange

C   Fill each gap with a suitable naming word.

1   a lovely ____   5   a quiet ____

2   a naughty ____   6   a clean ____

3   a sunny ____   7   a clever ____

4   a wide ____   8   a wild ____

64

Same sound — different meaning

Look at the four pairs of words below.

The words in each pair have the same sound but are different in spelling and meaning.

son	Mr. Day has one **son** and one daughter.
sun	The **sun** rises in the east and sets in the west.
weak	The sick man was too **weak** to get up.
week	There are seven days in a **week**.
hair	**Hair** grows on your head.
hare	A **hare** is an animal very much like a rabbit.
pair	A **pair** is a set of two, like a pair of shoes.
pear	A **pear** is a sweet juicy fruit.

Fill each space with the right word.

1 Father bought a new ____ of shoes.

2 The heat of the ____ makes plants grow.

3 The woman had black curly ____ .

4 The school was closed for a ____ .

5 This ____ is not quite ripe.

6 The ____ has long ears and a short tail.

7 Mary was quite ____ after her long illness.

8 The farmer told his ____ to fetch a pitchfork.

Jane's new bicycle

Jane has a brand new bicycle. It was given to her by her Uncle Bob as a present on her seventh birthday.

The bicycle is painted bright orange. Behind the seat is a black, plastic saddle-bag and there is a large, shiny bell on the handlebars.

Every evening Jane rides her bicycle down the lane behind her house. She goes to meet her father on his way home from work.

1   Who gave Jane the new bicycle?

2   How old was she when she was given the new bicycle?

3   Where is the saddle-bag?

4   What is the saddle-bag made of?

5   What is on the handlebars?

6   How often does Jane ride the bicycle?

7   Where is the lane where Jane rides?

8   Why does she ride down the lane?

Rhymes

The wind

What way does the wind come?
    What way does he go?
He rides over the water, and over the snow,
Through wood and through vale;
    and, o'er rocky height
Which the goat cannot climb,
    takes his sounding flight.
He tosses about in every bare tree,
As, if you look up, you plainly may see;
But how he will come, and whither he goes,
There's never a scholar in England knows.

Dorothy Wordsworth

A

1 Which word rhymes with **see**?

2 The word **goes** rhymes with ____?

3 Does **height** rhyme with **flight**?

4 Write the word which rhymes with **snow**.

5 Do the words **snow** and **knows** rhyme?

B   Write two words which rhyme with each of the words in bold type. The sentences will help you to find them.

snow   James had a ____ and arrow.
              We looked high and ____ for the bat.

flight   Jill had all her sums ____ .
              She goes to bed early every ____ .

tree   Robert fell down and cut his ____ .
              He was away from school for ____ days

knows   Mr. Gardener ____ lovely roses.
              He ____ them to all his friends.

Rhymes

A   Write this poem in your book.
Use the words in the list on the left to fill the spaces.

Sleep

bed   girls
feet   night
sack   still
back   alight
will   street
said   curls

In the dark and lonely ___ ,
When the stars are all ___ ,
Sleep comes creeping up the ___ ,
With her naked, silent ___ ,
Carrying upon her ___ ,
Dreams of all kinds in a ___ ;
Though the doors are bolted, ___
She can enter where she ___ ,
And she lingers, it is ___ ,
Longest by the children's ___ ;
Smooths their pillows, strokes their ___ ,
Happy little boys and ___ !

B   Write one word which rhymes with each pair below. For the first word you could choose from:

fed led red shed dead head bread tread

1 bed   said ___   4 still   will ___

2 feet street ___   5 night bite ___

3 back sack ___   6 try   lie ___

68

Using did and done

Pam **did** all the work.

Pam **has done** all the work.

(**has** helps the word **done**)

All the work **was done** by Pam.

(**was** helps the word **done**)

The word **did** needs no helping word.

The word **done** always has a helping word:

has done
have done
is done
are done
was done
were done
had done

A   Use **did** or **done** to fill each space.

1 I ____

2 You have ____

3 It was ____

4 He ____

5 You ____

6 He has ____

7 We ____

8 They are ____

9 She ____

10 We had ____

B   Fill each space with **did** or **done**.

1 Sally ____ her best to finish her homework.

2 We have ____ some good work today.

3 The soldier ____ his duty.

4 This drawing was ____ by Robert.

5 Robert ____ this drawing himself.

6 The gardener has ____ the lawns.

7 When the cakes are ____ you may have one.

8 When I was ill Jean ____ the cooking.

9 Polly ____ some gardening and then she went out.

10 After Polly had ____ some gardening she went out.

Jumbled sentences

The words in this sentence are not in their right order.

a has tail monkey The long

This sentence has the words in their right order.

The monkey has a long tail.

Put the words in these sentences in their correct order.

The capital letter shows which word comes first.

Put a full stop at the end of each sentence.

1 sheep We from wool the get

2 climbing girl is a tree The

3 grass is The cow some eating

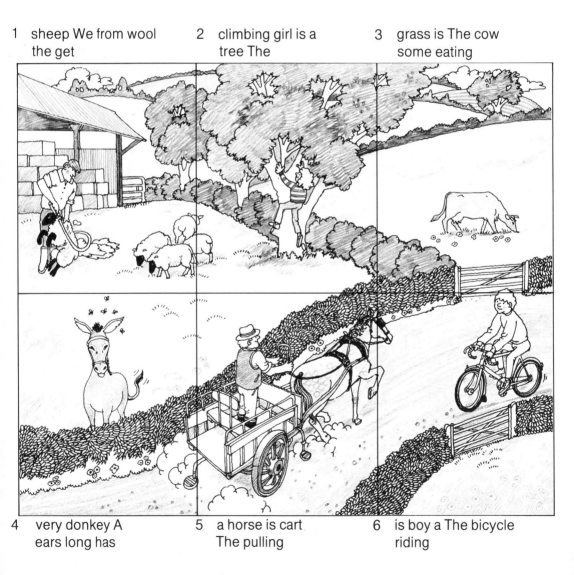

4 very donkey A ears long has

5 a horse is cart The pulling

6 is boy a The bicycle riding

70

Telling the time

The **little hand** of a clock or watch is called the **hour hand**.

The **big hand** is called the **minute hand**.

When the big hand points to **12**, it says **o'clock**.

This is three o'clock.

Write these times.

When the big hand points to **6**, it says **half past**.

This is half past nine.

Write these times.

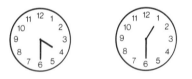

When the big hand points to **3**, it says **quarter past**.

This is quarter past six.

Write these times.

When the big hand points to **9**, it says **quarter to**.

This is quarter to three.

Write these times.

Making a snowman

A short time ago David and his friends John and Peter made a fine snowman. First they made a very big snowball for the head. Then David got a shovel and made a huge pile of snow for the body. Next, John and Peter put the head on top of the body. For eyes they used two bits of coal, and for the nose they used a carrot. Then Peter cut a long slit for the mouth.

John stuck an old clay pipe in the snowman's mouth, and Peter put an old bowler hat on its head. When they had finished making him they named him Sammy Snowball.

1 Which part of the snowman did the boys make first?

2 How did David make the body?

3 Who put the head on the body?

4 What did they use for eyes?

5 What was the carrot used for?

6 What did John stick in the snowman's mouth?

7 What did Peter put on the snowman's head?

8 What did they name the snowman?

A day in Ann's life

Copy each sentence in your book.
Fill in the time shown by each clock.

1   Ann woke at ....

2   She got up at ....

3   Ann was dressed by ....

4   She had breakfast at ....

5   Ann got to school at ....

6   She went out to play at ....

7   Ann left school at ....

8   She had tea at ....

Where they live

Learn the names of the homes of these creatures.

Write the missing words.

Creature	Home
bee	hive
bird	nest
dog	kennel
horse	stable
parrot	cage
pig	sty
rabbit	burrow
spider	web

1 A parrot lives in a ____ .

2 A ____ is the home of a spider.

3 The horse lives in a ____ .

4 A ____ is a dog's home.

5 Bees live in a ____ .

6 A pig lives in a ____ .

7 The rabbit lives in a ____ .

8 A bird lives in a ____ .

Describing words

A Use the words in the list on the left to describe the things below.

bright
fresh
happy
wooden
sharp
china
juicy
heavy

1 a _____ parcel
2 a _____ egg
3 a _____ star
4 a _____ teapot
5 a _____ knife
6 a _____ baby
7 a _____ orange
8 a _____ stool

B From the words in the list on the left choose the one which will best fit each line.

Example
1 The washing on the line is **clean**.
So the word **clean** fits line 1.

fine
stale
rich
clean
new
tidy
ripe
quiet

1 The washing on the line is _____ .

2 A pear which is ready for eating is _____ .

3 A person who has a lot of money is _____ .

4 A child who makes no noise is _____ .

5 A day when there is no rain is _____ .

6 Bread which was baked a week ago is _____ .

7 A dress which has never been worn is _____ .

8 A room in which nothing is out of place is _____

75

Hidden words

A Use a word of two letters to fill the gap in each of these sentences.

Example

1 At the seaside the children played in the s _ _d

Answer **an** s**an**d

1 At the seaside the children played in the s _ _ d.

2 The box was too heavy for Tom to l _ _ t.

3 The man struck a m _ _ ch to light his pipe.

4 Hot weather makes the butter very s _ _ t.

5 He did not have a w _ _ k of sleep last night.

6 Tony's coat was d _ _ p after the rain.

7 Martin caught a big f _ _ h with his new rod.

8 Six ducks were swimming on the p _ _ d.

9 Paul came l _ _ t in the race.

10 There were all s _ _ ts of toys in the shop.

B A word of three letters is hidden in each of the words in bold type. Find the ten words.

1 **grate**
an animal

2 **soaked**
a tree

3 **plant**
a small insect

4 **scarf**
we travel in it

5 **shears**
we listen with it

6 **scowl**
a big animal

7 **champion**
something to eat

8 **steal**
something to drink

9 **beggar**
we get it from a hen

10 **clipper**
a part of your mouth

Matching parts of sentences

Here you see two parts of a sentence.

Jane went to bed early   because she was so tired.

The first part tells what Jane did.

The second part tells why she did it.

Each sentence below is in two parts, but the parts have become mixed up.

Write the first part of each sentence then add on the part which fits it.

The leaves were falling	a very long neck.
Tony and Sheila	is called a lamb.
The cat lapped up	go to the seaside.
Our baby likes	are brother and sister.
The rabbit has	is called a stable.
A baby sheep	from the trees.
People often catch cold	a short furry tail.
A giraffe has	all the milk in the dish.
The home of a horse	playing with his rattle.
In summer many people	in very wet weather.

In the garden

Penny and Philip Hall often help their parents in the garden. Penny digs up the weeds which grow among the plants with a small fork. She puts them in a barrow. When the barrow is full, Philip wheels it down the path to the bottom of the garden. Then he throws all the weeds on a big heap to be burnt by his father.

Every Saturday Mrs. Hall cuts the lawn with a mower and trims the hedges with a pair of shears. She also likes to look after the flowers. When they are in bloom she often picks some and puts them in vases in the house. Mr. Hall grows all the vegetables. These include potatoes, carrots, cabbages and runner beans.

1 Who digs up the weeds in the garden?

2 How does Philip take the weeds down to the bottom of the garden?

3 What does Mr. Hall do with the weeds?

4 Who uses the lawn-mower?

5 What does Mrs. Hall use for trimming the hedges?

6 Who looks after the flowers?

7 What happens to the flowers when they are in bloom?

8 What vegetables are grown in the garden?

Rhymes

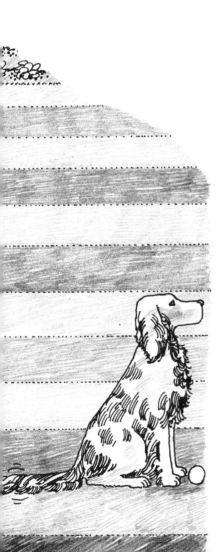

A In each group below write four words which rhyme with the word in bold type. The first letter of each new word is given.

1 **bat**
h _ _
m _ _
c _ _
f _ _

2 **cap**
l _ _
t _ _
m _ _
r _ _

3 **din**
f _ _
w _ _
p _ _
b _ _

4 **rut**
c _ _
n _ _
b _ _
h _ _

5 **best**
v _ _ _
n _ _ _
r _ _ _
w _ _ _

6 **lash**
d _ _ _
m _ _ _
c _ _ _
s _ _ _

7 **tent**
b _ _ _
s _ _ _
l _ _ _
r _ _ _

8 **meat**
s _ _ _
h _ _ _
b _ _ _
n _ _ _

9 **lack**
p _ _ _
s _ _ _
r _ _ _
b _ _ _

B Use a word which rhymes with **came** to fill the space in each sentence.

1 The horse was _ _ _ _ and could not run in the race.

2 The dog's _ _ _ _ was Bimbo.

3 Cricket is the _ _ _ _ I like best.

4 The candle _ _ _ _ is yellow.

5 The twins wear the _ _ _ _ kinds of clothes.

6 The keeper stroked the lion cub which was quite _ _ _ _.

7 The _ _ _ _ of the picture was made of wood.

8 Judy took the _ _ _ _ for the broken window.

Describing words adding -er and -est

long

longer

longest

When we add **-er** or **-est** to a word ending with **e**, we drop the **e**.

wide

wider

widest

A   Add **-er** or **-est** to the words in bold type to fill the spaces.

1   Andrew is much ____ than Derek.   **tall**

2   The church is the ____ building in town.   **high**

3   Carol has the ____ writing in the class.   **neat**

4   In winter we wear the ____ clothes we have.   **warm**

5   I am ____ than my brother James.   **old**

6   This knife is ____ than yours.   **sharp**

B

Add **-er** or **est** to the words in bold type to fill the gaps.

1   The weather is much ____ today.   **fine**

2   This is the ____ jam I have ever tasted.   **nice**

3   The pear was ____ than the banana.   **ripe**

4   The old lion was the ____ of the lot.   **tame**

5   King Solomon was the ____ of all men.   **wise**

6   She is much ____ after her illness.   **pale**

Beginning and ending sentences

A   Here are the beginnings of eight sentences. Finish each sentence yourself. Write them in your book.

1   The baby started crying ....

2   The car was badly damaged ....

3   At the end of our street ....

4   When tea was over ....

5   The cawing of the rooks ....

6   Mother sent for the doctor ....

7   Jane fed the puppy ....

8   The noise of the planes ....

B   Here are the endings of eight sentences. Write the first part of each in your own words.

1   .... so he went to bed.

2   .... and closed the door after him.

3   .... because of the heavy rain.

4   .... many trees lose their leaves.

5   .... but could not do it.

6   .... and put it in her purse.

7   .... when her kitten got lost.

8   .... and cut his knee.

Similars

Some words mean much the same as other words.

A **wealthy** man
A **rich** man

The words **wealthy** and **rich** are **similar**, or **alike**, in meaning.

Learn these similars, then do the exercises.

assist	help
broad	wide
correct	right
dwelling	home
farewell	goodbye
gaze	look
raise	lift
repair	mend
reply	answer
wealthy	rich

A   In place of each word in bold type, write a word which has a similar meaning.

1   The main street was very **broad**.

2   We stopped to **gaze** in the shop window.

3   Colin could hardly **raise** his arm.

4   The cobbler will **repair** my shoes today.

5   Will you **assist** me with my sums?

6   The duke is a very **wealthy** man.

7   William had all his sums **correct**.

8   The **reply** to the question was very short.

9   The shepherd's **dwelling** was a small cottage.

10   The sailor said **farewell** to his wife.

B   For each word below write one which is similar in meaning.

1	home	5	help
2	goodbye	6	answer
3	lift	7	mend
4	rich	8	wide

Joining sentences using and

Read these two sentences.

Simon is going fishing.
I am going fishing.

We can join these sentences
by using **and**

Simon **and** I are going fishing.

Here are more joined
sentences.

John is tall.
John is strong.

John is tall **and** strong.

Mary put her toys away.
She went to bed.

Mary put her toys away **and** went to bed.

Use **and** to join each pair of sentences below.

1   Our cat is white.
    Our cat is fluffy.

2   The room was clean.
    The room was tidy.

3   Grandpa sat in the armchair.
    He fell fast asleep.

4   The day was fine.
    The day was warm.

5   I gave the grocer fifty pence.
    I had five pence change.

6   The farmer ploughs the fields.
    He sows the seed.

7   We went to the park.
    We played ball.

8   The nurse took my temperature.
    The nurse took my pulse.

9   John had his breakfast.
    John went to school.

I saw a ship a-sailing

I saw a ship a-sailing,
    A-sailing on the sea;
And it was deeply laden
    With pretty things for me.

There were raisins in the cabin
    And almonds in the hold;
The sails were made of satin,
    And the mast was made of gold.

The four and twenty sailors
    Who stood upon the decks
Were four and twenty white mice
    With rings about their necks.

The captain was a fine plump duck
    With a jacket on his back,
And when the fairy ship set sail
    The captain he said Quack!

1 Where were the raisins?

2 What were the sails made of?

3 What part of the ship was made of gold?

4 How many sailors stood on the decks?

5 Who were the sailors?

6 Who was the captain?

7 What did he have on his back?

8 What did the captain say when the ship set sail?

Things which are alike

When something is very **heavy** we say it is as **heavy** as **lead**.

This is because lead is a very, very heavy metal.

Learn the sayings in this list, then answer the questions below.

as cold as ice

as good as gold

as heavy as lead

as light as a feather

as quiet as a mouse

as slow as a snail

as sweet as honey

as thin as a rake

as warm as toast

as white as snow

A

1 as cold as _____

2 as white as _____

3 as good as _____

4 as warm as _____

5 as thin as a _____

6 as heavy as _____

7 as light as a _____

8 as sweet as _____

9 as quiet as a _____

10 as slow as a _____

B   Use the right word to finish each sentence.

1 The baby's toes were as _____ as toast.

2 The grapes were as _____ as honey.

3 David was as _____ as gold in school.

4 The tea was as _____ as ice.

5 Her hair was as _____ as snow.

6 The newspaper boy was as _____ as a snail.

7 This box is as _____ as a feather.

8 After his illness he was as _____ as a rake.

THE QUIET MOUSE

Describing words adding -er and -est

When we add **-er** or **-est** to some words we **double the last letter**.

big   bigger   biggest

When we add **-er** or **-est** to words ending with **y** we change the **y** to **i**.

easy   easier   easiest

A

Add **-er** or **-est** to the words in bold type to fill the spaces.

1   This is the ＿＿ day for years.   **hot**

2   Holland is a ＿＿ country than England.   **flat**

3   Friday was the ＿＿ day of the week.   **wet**

4   He picked the ＿＿ slice of cake on the plate.   **thin**

5   The clown's nose was ＿＿ than a cherry.   **red**

6   It was the ＿＿ day of his life.   **sad**

B

1   John is the ＿＿ boy in the whole world.   **happy**

2   Martin seems to be ＿＿ than his brother.   **lazy**

3   The rose is a ＿＿ flower than the dandelion.   **pretty**

4   Her bedroom is the ＿＿ room in the house.   **tidy**

5   The boys are ＿＿ than the girls.   **noisy**

6   Christmas is the ＿＿ time of year.   **merry**

Joining sentences using but

Read these two sentences.

Carol dropped her clock.
It did not break.

We can join these sentences
by using **but**.

Carol dropped her clock **but** it did not break.

See how these other sentences
are joined.

Paul fell down.
He did not cry.

Paul fell down **but** he did not cry.

The dog chased a rabbit.
He did not catch it.

The dog chased a rabbit **but** he did not catch it.

Use **but** to join each pair of sentences below.

1 Jill looked for her lost book.
   She could not find it.

2 We hoped to go out.
   It was too wet.

3 Tim fell off his scooter.
   He did not hurt himself.

4 The postman rang the bell.
   He could not get an answer.

5 They hurried to the station.
   The train had gone.

6 Sandra felt ill.
   She did not want to stay in bed.

7 Ann wanted a chocolate.
   The box was empty.

8 I longed for some ice-cream.
   I had no money.

9 We went into the park.
   We did not stay long.

Using saw and seen

William **saw** a lion.

(**saw** needs no helping word)

William **had seen** a lion before.

(**had** helps the word **seen**)

We **have seen** lions at the zoo.

(**have** helps the word **seen**)

The word **saw** needs no helping word.

The word **seen** always has a helping word:

has seen
have seen
is seen
are seen
was seen
were seen
had seen

A Use **saw** or **seen** to fill each space.

1 She ____
2 They were ____
3 I ____
4 She had ____
5 We ____
6 I have ____
7 They ____
8 It is ____
9 You ____
10 He was ____

B Which is right, **saw** or **seen**?

1 The wise men had ____ a bright star in the sky.

2 I ____ a giant at the fair.

3 Have you ____ the new car?

4 James ____ the football match from start to finish.

5 The policeman ____ a man breaking into a shop.

6 The robber was ____ by the policeman.

7 The robber did not know that he had been ____ .

8 I thought I ____ you at the party.

9 I knew I had ____ you before.

10 Crocuses are ____ in the spring.

Looking back

A   Write the **opposites** of:

1	top	4	pretty	7	clean
2	full	5	wrong	8	fresh
3	late	6	tame		

B   Write the words for **more than one**.

1	leaf	4	wife	7	coach
2	baby	5	story	8	lady
3	box	6	brush		

C   Add **-est** to each of these describing words.

1	clean	4	ripe	7	fine
2	big	5	hot	8	thin
3	happy	6	long		

D   Name the **homes** of these creatures.

1	spider	4	robin	7	horse
2	parrot	5	pig	8	bees
3	lion	6	dog		

E   Write words which are **similar** in meaning.

1	speak	4	wealthy	7	large
2	broad	5	correct	8	repair
3	begin	6	stout		

F   Write words which **sound** like these but have different spellings.

1	made	4	won	7	our
2	not	5	by	8	new
3	tail	6	see		

Going for a picnic

One hot day in September Mr. and Mrs. Brown took their three children, Peter, Sally and Julie for a picnic in the woods.

While the children searched for conkers their parents put out cold sausages, potato salad and tins of Coke. Then Mrs. Brown opened a box of cakes she had made the day before.

Suddenly, there was a shriek from Julie. "Quick, Daddy! An adder!" she cried.

Mr. Brown sprang to his feet and ran to Julie. Then he laughed, "Don't worry, Julie," he said, "It's only a grass snake."

1 Where did they go for a picnic?

2 How many children did Mr. and Mrs. Brown have?

3 What did the children do when they reached the woods?

4 What did they all have to drink?

5 Who had made the cakes?

6 When had they been made?

7 Why did Julie shriek?

8 What did Mr. Brown see when he went to look?

ANSWERS

Page 1 The game of I spy

A

1	cup	6	log
2	peg	7	tree
3	boat	8	fish
4	sock	9	jug
5	dog	10	egg

B

1	egg
2	dog
3	fish
4	sock

Page 2 Names of things

A

1	bed	6	book
2	pen	7	drum
3	door	8	clock
4	tap	9	spoon
5	lamp	10	bag

B

1	drum	6	book
2	bed	7	tap
3	lamp	8	spoon
4	door	9	pen
5	bag	10	clock

Page 3 Using a and an

A

1 an egg-cup
2 an axe
3 an arrow
4 an oven
5 an iron
6 an envelope
7 an apple
8 an onion

B

1 a clock
2 an armchair
3 an orchard
4 a book
5 a pen
6 an arch
7 a tree
8 a door
9 an elephant
10 an ostrich
11 an eagle
12 a hoop
13 a desk
14 an island
15 an umbrella

Page 4 Numbers

1	three cats	4	one car	7	eight flowers	10	seven bottles
2	five spoons	5	four apples	8	nine pencils		
3	two trees	6	ten eggs	9	six mugs		

Page 5 Doing words

A

1 flying
2 eating
3 reading
4 fishing
5 washing
6 drinking
7 jumping
8 sleeping

B

1 washing
2 sleeping
3 fishing
4 eating
5 reading
6 jumping
7 flying
8 drinking

C

1 calling
2 drawing
3 doing
4 trying
5 pulling
6 seeing
7 hearing
8 raining
9 singing
10 barking
11 teaching
12 feeling

Page 6 Pam's pet

1. Pam's cat is <u>black</u> in colour.
2. When Punch is <u>happy</u> he purrs.
3. Every day Pam gives her cat some <u>milk</u>.
4. He <u>laps</u> it up with his <u>long pink</u> tongue.
5. Punch <u>often</u> sits on the <u>rug</u> by the <u>fire</u>.
6. He washes his <u>face</u> with his <u>soft paws</u>.
7. His claws are very <u>sharp</u>.
8. Punch keeps <u>mice</u> away from the <u>house</u>.

Page 7 More doing words

A

1	hiding	5	riding
2	skating	6	diving
3	dancing	7	waving
4	writing	8	driving

B

1	riding	5	driving
2	hiding	6	diving
3	waving	7	dancing
4	writing	8	skating

Page 8 Telling sentences

A

1. Butter is made from milk.
2. Honey is made by bees.
3. Sugar has a sweet taste.
4. The school bus was late today.
5. Mary had dinner at school.
6. I put some coal on the fire.
7. We go blackberrying in the autumn.
8. The crocus is a spring flower.
9. The elephant has a long trunk.
10. A young cat is called a kitten.

B

Own answers.

Page 9 Asking sentences

A

1. How are you today?
2. Why were you late this morning?
3. Where did you put the sweets?
4. When are you coming to see me?
5. Who told you that I was ill?
6. Which of these toys do you like best?
7. Will you come to the circus with me?
8. Did you remember to post the letter?
9. Have you seen John?
10. Can you tell me the way?

B

Own answers.

Page 10 Capital letters beginning a sentence

A

1 Honey is sweet.
2 The sun sets in the west.
3 Do you like nuts?
4 A rabbit has soft fur.
5 When will you be ready?
6 Keep off the grass.
7 This meat is very tender.
8 Are you going shopping?
9 Look where you are going.
10 What is the right time?

B
Own answers.

Page 11 The alphabet

A

1 e
2 z
3 t
4 g
5 l
6 d f
7 s
8 h
9 o s v
10 beg

B

1 l m n o p
2 u v w x y
3 q r s t u v
4 a b c d e f
5 f g h i j k

Page 12 The Hall family

1 This is the Hall family.
2 There are five people in all.
3 The father is reading a book.
4 He is also eating a banana.
5 The mother is writing a letter.
6 The baby is sitting on the floor.
7 He has a ball in his hands.
8 The girl is playing with the cat.
9 The dog is asleep by the fire.
10 The boy is watching the television.

Page 13 Doing words

A

1 clapping
2 batting
3 running
4 cutting
5 sitting
6 skipping
7 chopping
8 swimming

B

1 slipping
2 digging
3 stopping
4 getting
5 rotting
6 putting
7 shutting
8 knitting

Page 14   Capital letters

A

1   I told Mary that I would play with her after tea.
2   When Peggy fell down Paul helped her up.
3   I think David Maggs is taller than John Perry.
4   The names of the twins are Pamela and Kenneth.
5   I saw Roy Bond feeding his dog Sam.
6   We saw Daisy the cow being milked.
7   Linda named her new pony Sunshine.
8   The name of our cat is Fluffy.

B
Write a capital I in each space.

Page 15   Names and initials

A

1   Mr. J. Cobb
2   Mr. H. Watts
3   Mr. D. R. Bond

B

1   Mrs. I. Bevan
2   Mrs. D. Gaye
3   Mrs. J. A. Davis

C

1   Miss J. Mason
2   Miss D. Eynon
3   Miss A. M. Carr

D

1   Dr. W. Penn
2   Dr. H. Taylor
3   Dr. M. I. Fox

Page 16   Numbers—the teens

1   thirteen
2   twelve
3   eleven
4   nineteen
5   seventeen
6   fifteen
7   fourteen

8   eighteen
9   twelve
10   sixteen
11   twelve; fourteen; sixteen; eighteen
12   eleven; thirteen; fifteen; seventeen; nineteen

Page 17   More than one

A

four shoes
three pigs

five keys
six frogs

two boats
seven apples

B

1   hens
4   pens
7   boats
10   sweets

2   cows
5   ducks
8   socks
11   caps

3   ships
6   horses
9   nuts
12   shoes

C

1	dogs	2	legs	3	girls
4	weeks	5	days	6	sweets
7	chocolates	8	cards	9	books
10	boys				

Page 18   Verses

A

1 The old man lives at the top of the street.
2 All day long he talks to his cat.
3 At night he puts on a big wide-awake hat.
4 The old man's beard reaches to his feet.

B

1 The vulture's neck is growing thinner.
2 His eye is dull and his head is bald.
3 He rarely feels as well as you or I.
4 This is because he eats between meals.

Page 19   He and she

A

1	Lady	5	wife
2	aunt	6	queen
3	woman	7	sister
4	nephew	8	girl

B

1	husband	5	brother
2	lord	6	prince
3	uncle	7	father
4	nephew	8	king

Page 20   Days of the week

1	Tuesday	2	Wednesday	3	Saturday; Sunday
4	Thursday	5	Wednesday	6	Monday
7	Sunday	8	Saturday	9	Wednesday
10	Saturday				

Page 21   More than one

A

1	bushes	6	peaches
2	watches	7	dishes
3	coaches	8	churches
4	brushes	9	torches
5	boxes	10	matches

B

1	watches	6	coaches
2	bushes	7	brushes
3	churches	8	boxes
4	dishes	9	peaches
5	matches	10	torches

Page 22   Capital letters

A

1. London is the capital of England.
2. Ships sail from Dover.
3. He was born in Oxford.
4. Bath is a very old city.
5. Jane lives in Ashton Road, Bristol.
6. We went by train to York.
7. The liner docked in Liverpool.
8. The biggest city in Wales is Cardiff.
9. Many people visit Windsor Castle.
10. He has moved from Station Road to Oak Avenue.

B
Own answers.

Page 23   To, two and too

1 to	2 two; two	3 too; to; to	4 two
5 to	6 to	7 too; to	8 two
9 to; too	10 too; to		

Page 24   Busy Children

1. There are five children in the picture.
2. Two of them are boys and three are girls.
3. Roger has made a rabbit out of clay.
4. Susan has done a drawing and is showing it to Alan.
5. There is a jar of water in front of Alan.
6. Mary is painting a picture of a house.
7. Her picture is standing on the easel.
8. Ann has a set of coloured pencils.
9. Alan sits at the end of the table. (Also Ann)
10. Mary is the only child standing.

Page 25   Numbers the tens

A

1 seventy	2 fifty	3 forty	4 sixty
5 thirty			

B

a forty-two	b ninety-seven	c seventy-eight	d fifty-four
e eighty-three	f twenty-nine	g ninety-four	h eighty-five
i thirty-eight			

Page 26   Colours

A

1	yellow	2	green	3	black	4	red
5	brown	6	red	7	yellow	8	white
9	red	10	white				

B

Own answers.

C

1	green	2	red	3	green	4	yellow
5	white	6	blue	7	black	8	brown
9	red	10	grey; white				

Page 27   More than one

A

1	flies	2	ponies	3	puppies	4	berries
5	daisies	6	gipsies	7	stories	8	fairies
9	babies	10	ladies				

B

1	berries	2	babies	3	puppies	4	ponies
5	stories	6	gipsies	7	flies	8	fairies

Page 28   More than one

A

1	ten thieves	2	three shelves	3	five loaves	4	two halves
5	four calves	6	many leaves	7	ten sheaves	8	a pack of wolves
9	wives	10	lives	11	knives		

B

1	shelves	2	loaves	3	leaves	4	halves
5	calves	6	Wolves	7	knives	8	thieves

Page 29   Adding -ed to doing words

A

1	rained	2	played	3	chewed	4	waited
5	asked	6	barked	7	filled	8	picked
9	opened	10	fetched				

B

1	asked	2	picked	3	barked	4	fetched
5	played	6	waited	7	filled	8	rained
9	chewed	10	opened				

Page 30 Martin's toys

1 Martin keeps his toys in a big cupboard.
2 Some of them are new but most of them are old.
3 Martin likes his clockwork train best of all.
4 The oldest toy is a teddy bear.
5 Martin had it when he was a year old.
6 His mother bought it for him.
7 The teddy bear was a birthday present from his mother.
8 The crane can lift the tractor right off the floor.

Page 31 Using is and are/Using was and were

A
1 is   2 Is   3 is   4 Is
   are   Are   are   Are

B
1 was   2 was   3 Was   4 was
   were   were   Were   were

C
1 is; is   2 were; was   3 was; was   4 is; are   5 were; was

Page 32 The alphabet

A
bin
bucket
caravan
fork
gate
house
ladder
post

B
1 an   be   do   if   pan   so
2 add   big   car   day   end   fat
3 bit   job   low   one   son   two
4 arm   bag   eye   got   use   why

C
1 gun   2 zoo   3 cow   4 wet   5 bell

Page 33 Doing words—past time

A
1 sneezed   2 liked   3 wiped
4 fired   5 hoped   6 waved
7 used   8 dived   9 saved
10 joked   11 baked   12 moved

B

1	sneezed	2	moved	3	waved
4	fired	5	dived	6	used
7	saved	8	liked	9	wiped
10	joked				

Page 34   Adding-ed to doing words

A

1 pinned
2 clapped
3 stopped
4 begged
5 tapped
6 hugged
7 wagged
8 chopped
9 hummed
10 sipped

B

1 begged
2 wagged
3 sipped
4 stopped
5 hugged
6 tapped
7 pinned
8 chopped
9 clapped
10 hummed

Page 35   Putting sentences in order

1

c James went into the sweet shop.
e He asked for a packet of mints.
a He paid the shopkeeper.
d He put the change in his pocket.
b He joined his friends outside.

2

d Wendy took a bottle of milk from the crate.
e She took off the cap.
b She put a straw in the bottle.
a She drank all the milk.
c She put the empty bottle in the crate.

3

e Michael got out of bed at eight o'clock.
a He went to the bathroom to wash himself.
d He dressed himself and went downstairs.
c He ate his breakfast and left the table.
b He went off to catch the school bus.

4

d The rocket landed safely on the moon.
c Two spacemen climbed out of the rocket.
a They walked about collecting moon rocks.
e The spacemen climbed back into their rocket.
b The rocket took off from the moon with a loud blast from its engines.

Page 36 Going to school

1 The name of Ann's brother is John Dawes.
2 Yes, John and Ann go to the same school.
3 Ann is in Class 1.
4 They live quite near the school.
5 Before going to school every morning John takes his dog for a long walk.
6 His sister feeds her two rabbits.
7 Snowy is white; Sooty is black.
8 Mrs. Davies is the lollipop lady. She sees that the children cross the road safely.

Page 37 Opposites using un

A

1	unlock	2	unpaid	3	unwell	4	unpack
5	unkind	6	undo	7	unscrew	8	unwind
9	unknown	10	untie	11	unload	12	unwrap

B
Own answers.

C

1	undress	2	untidy	3	unfit	4	untrue
5	unable	6	unhappy	7	unwilling	8	unsafe

Page 38 Opposites—change of words

1	old	2	good	3	early	4	weak
5	cold	6	soft	7	out	8	short
9	shut	10	tame				

Page 39 Adding -ed to doing words

A

1	dried	2	carried	3	copied	4	tidied
5	cried	6	buried	7	hurried	8	fried
9	emptied						

B

1	hurried	2	fried	3	cried	4	carried
5	dried	6	tidied	7	buried	8	copied
9	paid						

Page 40 Two word games

	A		B
1	pink	1	lift
2	hold	2	chin
3	spin	3	leaf
4	learn	4	race
5	price	5	each
6	beach	6	team
7	broom	7	last
8	beast	8	over

Page 41 Using is and his/Using as and has

	A		B
1	is	1	has
2	his	2	as; as
3	his	3	as
4	is	4	has
5	His; is	5	as
6	is; his	6	Has
7	is; is	7	has; as; as
8	his; his	8	has; as; as

Page 42 Little Robin Redbreast

1 Robin sat upon a *tree*.
2 Robin *sang* as merrily as could be.
3 He *nodded* with his head.
4 He waggled his *tail*.
5 Robin has a scarlet *breast*.
6 In the *winter* his nest is cold.
7 Robin hops on the *carpet* and picks up the *crumbs*.
8 Robin knows the *children* love him when he *comes*.

Page 43   Roger and Pam

A
1. On his head Roger wears a *bobble-hat*.
2. His *anorak* keeps the wind out.
3. On his feet he wears blue *shoes*.
4. Under his anorak he wears a *sweater*.
5. Roger wears a *belt* to keep his jeans up.

B
1. Pam wears a check *jacket*.
2. Round her neck she wears a long woolly *scarf*.
3. On her feet she wears blue *boots*.
4. She wears a blue pleated *skirt*.
5. Pam wears *gloves* to keep her hands warm.

Page 44   Things we eat and drink

	A		B
1	bananas	1	packet
2	chocolate	2	loaf
3	sardines	3	pot
4	milk	4	cup
5	tea	5	bottle
6	biscuits	6	bunch
7	jam	7	bar
8	bread	8	tin

Page 45   Rhymes

A

1	man / can	2	bee / sea	3	tale / sail	4	seat / meet
5	bear / hair	6	late / wait				

B

1	trip / ship	2	sore / four	3	mill / fill	4	down / brown
5	line / fine	6	peel / seal	7	peas / bees	8	pull / full
9	hard / card	10	farm / harm				

Page 46 Using has and have

A

1 has	2 have	3 have	4 has
5 Has	6 Have	7 have	8 Has
9 has	10 have		

B
Own answers.

Page 47 Words with more than one meaning

1 back	2 calf	3 post	4 lean
5 mine	6 band	7 left	8 stick
9 suit			

Page 48 In the woods

1 Carol and Mary *went* for a *walk* in the *woods* one day.
2 They *took* their dog *Sammy* with *them*.
3 Sammy *ran* on in front of *them*.
4 Sammy *knew* the way.
   He had *been* there *many* times *before*.
5 The children *found* some *bluebells* growing.
6 They *picked* a *bunch* for their *mother*.
7 Sammy saw a *rabbit* sitting *under* a *tree*.
8 He ran *after* it but did not *catch* it.

Page 49 Same sound—different meaning

1 won	2 tale	3 buy	4 one
5 made	6 tail	7 by	8 maid

Page 50 People who work

A

1 milkman	2 postman	3 doctor	4 farmer
5 baker	6 grocer	7 miner	8 zoo keeper

B

1 postman	2 butcher	3 doctor	4 milkman
5 miner	6 zoo keeper	7 pilot	8 baker
9 dustman	10 grocer		

Page 51 The not words

A
1 doesn't
2 weren't
3 hasn't
4 isn't
5 haven't
6 wasn't
7 don't
8 aren't

B
1 doesn't
2 weren't
3 hasn't
4 isn't
5 Wasn't
6 don't
7 haven't
8 aren't

Page 52 Using do and does

A
1 does
2 do
3 do
4 does
5 do
6 does

B
1 don't
2 doesn't
3 doesn't
4 don't
5 don't
6 doesn't

Page 53 Capital letters

A

1 London	2 George	3 Friday	4 Thomson
5 France	6 Nelson	7 Thames	8 Betty
9 April	10 Monday	11 England	12 Jones
13 Arthur	14 July		

B
1 Did you know that I was seven last Sunday?
2 Linda and Charles live in Church Street.
3 Roy goes to Brighton every Saturday.
4 I take my dog Chum for a walk every day.
5 Jack and Jill went up the hill.
6 Farmer Grey has a cow named Daisy.
7 We shall be moving to Bristol next Tuesday.
8 The Severn is the longest river in England.

Page 54 Children at play

1 David is on roller *skates*.
2 He is going very *fast*.
3 Betty and Ann are having a *skipping* race.
4 Roger and James are playing *marbles*.

5 James is *holding* a marble in his right hand.
6 Jill is on the *swing*.
7 The swing hangs from a *branch* of the tree.
8 The trunk of the tree is very *thick*.

Page 55 Joining words

A
Own answers.

B
1	milkman	2	windmill	3	seaside	4	dustbin
5	hatband	6	handbag	7	pigsty	8	bedroom
9	football	10	doorbell				

Page 56 Doing words—past time

A

1	drew	7	break	
2	drank	8	hide	
3	bit	9	creep	
4	flew	10	did	
5	come	11	fall	
6	wear	12	gave	

B

1 hid
2 gave
3 flew
4 bit
5 drew
6 broke
7 did
8 wore

Page 57 Opposites—change of word

A

1	pretty	7	up
2	thick	8	top
3	right	9	clean
4	over	10	begin
5	fresh	11	wet
6	give	12	low

B

1	down	6	stale
2	finish	7	give
3	dirty	8	under
4	bottom	9	thin
5	wrong	10	ugly

Page 58 Same sound—different meaning

1	new	2	sea	3	not
4	knew	5	our	6	see; sea
7	not; knot	8	hour		

Page 59   Collections

	A		B
1	chocolates	1	bunch
2	people	2	herd
3	flowers	3	pack
4	trees	4	crowd
5	cards	5	flock
6	tools	6	clump
7	elephants	7	box
8	sheep	8	set

Page 60   Sausages for supper

1 Rachel has her favourite food once a week (every Saturday).
2 Her mother fries the sausages.
3 The chips are golden in colour.
4 Rachel usually has two helpings.
5 Rachel's pudding is served in a large bowl.
6 The two colours are pink and brown.
7 There are four pieces of wafer in her sailing-boat.
8 Rachel would like sausages and chips every day.

Page 61   Showing ownership

1 *Ian's* bat
2 *Sarah's* teddy bear
3 *Ann's* ball
4 *Peter's* top
5 *Alan's* car
6 *Janet's* pram
7 *David's* scooter
8 *Pam's* cat

Page 62   Groups

A

Animals	Birds	Trees	Flowers
sheep	robin	beech	tulip
pig	thrush	oak	daisy
cow	rook	fir	pansy
goat	lark	elm	rose

B

Tools	Clothes	Furniture	Colours
spanner	coat	table	green
hammer	shirt	chair	yellow
axe	shorts	settee	blue
saw	jersey	wardrobe	brown

Page 63   Similars

A

1	begin	6	stop
2	crawl	7	fat
3	pull	8	rip
4	big	9	gift
5	talk	10	end

B

1	large	5	present
2	speak	6	creep
3	finish	7	halt
4	tug	8	start

Page 64   Describing words

A

1 savage
2 shady
3 rough
4 gold
5 silk
6 blazing
7 tasty
8 fast
9 kind
10 sour

B
Own answers.

C
Own answers.

Page 65   Same sound—different meaning

1	pair	2	sun	3	hair	4	week
5	pear	6	hare	7	weak	8	son

Page 66   Jane's new bicycle

1 Her Uncle Bob gave Jane her new bicycle.
2 Jane was seven when she was given the new bicycle.
3 The saddle-bag is behind the seat.
4 The saddle-bag is made of plastic.
5 On the handle-bars is a large, shiny bell.
6 Jane rides her bicycle every day.
7 The lane where she rides is behind her house.
8 She rides down the lane to meet her father on his way home from work.

Page 67   Rhymes

A

1	tree	2	knows	3	Yes	4	go
5	No						

B

snow	bow
	low
flight	right
	night
tree	knee
	three
knows	grows
	shows

Page 68 Rhymes

A

1	night	2	alight	3	street	4	feet
5	back	6	sack	7	still	8	will
9	said	10	bed	11	curls	12	girls

B
Own answers.

Page 69 Using did and done

A

1	did	6	done
2	done	7	did
3	done	8	done
4	did	9	did
5	did	10	done

B

1	did	6	done
2	done	7	done
3	did	8	did
4	done	9	did
5	did	10	done

Page 70 Jumbled sentences

1 We get wool from the sheep.
2 The girl is climbing a tree.
3 The cow is eating some grass.
4 A donkey has very long ears.
5 The horse is pulling a cart.
6 The boy is riding a bicycle.

Page 71 Telling the time

eight o'clock	five o'clock	eleven o'clock
half past four	half past one	half past seven

Page 72   Making a snowman

1   The boys made the head of the snowman first.
2   David made a huge pile of snow for the body.
3   John and Peter put the head on the body.
4   The boys used two bits of coal for the eyes.
5   The carrot was used for the nose.
6   John stuck an old, clay pipe in the snowman's mouth.
7   Peter put an old, bowler hat on the snowman's head.
8   The boys named the snowman Sammy Snowball.

Page 73   A day in Ann's life

1   half past seven   2   quarter to eight   3   eight o'clock
4   quarter past eight   5   nine o'clock   6   half past ten
7   four o'clock   8   quarter to five

Page 74   Where they live

1   cage   2   web   3   stable   4   kennel
5   hive   6   sty   7   burrow   8   nest

Page 75   Describing words

A
1   heavy   2   fresh   3   bright   4   china
5   sharp   6   happy   7   juicy   8   wooden

B
1   clean   2   ripe   3   rich   4   quiet
5   fine   6   stale   7   new   8   tidy

Page 76   Hidden words

A
1   an   2   if   3   at   4   of
5   in   6   am   7   is   8   on
9   as   10   or

B
1	rat	2	oak	3	ant	4	car
5	ear	6	cow	7	ham	8	tea
9	egg	10	lip				

Page 77   Matching parts of sentences

1 The leaves were falling from the trees.
2 Tony and Sheila are brother and sister.
3 The cat lapped up all the milk in the dish.
4 Our baby likes playing with his rattle.
5 The rabbit has a short, furry tail.
6 A baby sheep is called a lamb.
7 People often catch cold in very wet weather.
8 A giraffe has a very long neck.
9 The home of a horse is called a stable.
10 In summer many people go to the seaside.

Page 78   In the garden

1 Penny digs up the weeds in the garden.
2 Philip takes the weeds down to the bottom of the garden in a wheelbarrow.
3 Mr. Hall burns the weeds.
4 Mrs. Hall uses the lawn-mower.
5 Mrs. Hall uses a pair of shears for trimming the hedges.
6 Mrs. Hall looks after the flowers.
7 When the flowers are in bloom they are picked and put in vases in the house.
8 Potatoes, carrots, cabbages and runner beans are grown in the garden.

Page 79   Rhymes

A

1	hat	2	lap	3	fin
	mat		tap		win
	cat		map		pin
	fat		rap		bin
4	cut	5	vest	6	dash
	nut		nest		mash
	but		rest		cash
	hut		west		sash
7	bent	8	seat	9	pack
	sent		heat		sack
	lent		beat		rack
	rent		neat		back

B

1	lame	2	name	3	game	4	flame
5	same	6	tame	7	frame	8	blame

Page 80 Describing words—adding -er and -est

A
1 taller
2 highest
3 neatest
4 warmest
5 older
6 sharper

B
1 finer
2 nicest
3 riper
4 tamest
5 wisest
6 paler

Page 81 Beginning and ending sentences

A
Own answers.

B
Own answers.

Page 82 Similars

A
1 wide
2 look
3 lift
4 mend
5 help
6 rich
7 right
8 answer
9 home
10 goodbye

B
1 dwelling
2 farewell
3 raise
4 wealthy
5 assist
6 reply
7 repair
8 broad

Page 83 Joining sentences using and

1 Our cat is white and fluffy.
2 The room was clean and tidy.
3 Grandpa sat in the armchair and fell fast asleep.
4 The day was fine and warm.
5 I gave the grocer fifty pence and had five pence change.
6 The farmer ploughs the fields and sows the seed.
7 We went to the park and played ball.
8 The nurse took my temperature and my pulse.
9 John had his breakfast and went to school.

Page 84 I saw a ship a-sailing

1 The raisins were in the cabin.
2 The sails were made of satin.
3 The mast was made of gold.
4 Twenty-four sailors stood on the deck.
5 The sailors were white mice with rings about their necks.
6 The captain was a fine plump duck.
7 He had a jacket on his back.
8 The captain said Quack when the ship set sail.

Page 85 Things which are alike

A

1	ice	6	lead
2	snow	7	feather
3	gold	8	honey
4	toast	9	mouse
5	rake	10	snail

B

1	warm	5	white
2	sweet	6	slow
3	good	7	light
4	cold	8	thin

Page 86 Describing words—adding -er and -est

A

1 hottest
2 flatter
3 wettest
4 thinnest
5 redder
6 saddest

B

1 happiest
2 lazier
3 prettier
4 tidiest
5 noisier
6 merriest

Page 87 Joining sentences using but

1 Jill looked for her lost book but could not find it.
2 We hoped to go out but it was too wet.
3 Tim fell off his scooter but he did not hurt himself.
4 The postman rang the bell but could not get an answer.
5 They hurried to the station but the train had gone.
6 Sandra felt ill but she did not want to stay in bed.
7 Ann wanted a chocolate but the box was empty.
8 I longed for some ice-cream but I had no money.
9 We went into the park but we did not stay long.

Page 88 Using saw and seen

A

1	saw	6	seen
2	seen	7	saw
3	saw	8	seen
4	seen	9	saw
5	saw	10	seen

B

1	seen	6	seen
2	saw	7	seen
3	seen	8	saw
4	saw	9	seen
5	saw	10	seen

Page 89 Looking back

A

1 bottom
2 empty
3 early
4 ugly
5 right
6 wild
7 dirty
8 stale

B

1 leaves
2 babies
3 boxes
4 wives
5 stories
6 brushes
7 coaches
8 ladies

C

1 cleanest
2 biggest
3 happiest
4 ripest
5 hottest
6 longest
7 finest
8 thinnest

D

1 web
2 cage
3 den
4 nest
5 sty
6 kennel
7 stable
8 hive

E

1 talk
2 wide
3 start
4 rich
5 right
6 fat
7 big
8 mend

F

1 maid
2 knot
3 tale
4 one
5 buy
6 sea
7 hour
8 knew

Page 90 Going for a picnic

1 They went for a picnic in the woods.
2 Mr. and Mrs. Brown had three children.
3 When the children reached the woods they looked for conkers.
4 They had Coke to drink.
5 Mrs. Brown had made the cakes.
6 The cakes had been made the day before.
7 Julie shrieked because she saw what she thought was an adder.
8 When Mr. Brown went to look he saw that it was a grass snake.